RUDOLF STEINER (1861–1925) called his spiritual philosophy 'anthroposophy', meaning 'wisdom of the human being'. As a highly developed seer, he based his work on direct knowledge and perception of spiritual dimensions. He initiated a modern and universal 'science of spirit', accessible to anyone willing to exercise clear and unprejudiced thinking.

From his spiritual investigations Steiner provided suggestions for the renewal of many activities, including education (both general and special), agriculture, medicine, economics, architecture, science, philosophy, religion and the arts. Today there are thousands of schools, clinics, farms and other organizations involved in practical work based on his principles. His many published works feature his research into the spiritual nature of the human being, the evolution of the world and humanity, and methods of personal development. Steiner wrote some 30 books and delivered over 6,000 lectures across Europe. In 1924 he founded the General Anthroposophical Society, which today has branches throughout the world.

ANTHROPOSOPHICAL LEADING THOUGHTS

Anthroposophy as a Path of Knowledge

The Michael Mystery

RUDOLF STEINER

Translated by
George and Mary Adams

Rudolf Steiner Press

Rudolf Steiner Press
Hillside House, The Square
Forest Row, E. Sussex
RH18 5ES

www.rudolfsteinerpress.com

First edition Rudolf Steiner Press 1973
Reprinted 1985, 1998 and 2007

Originally published in German under the title *Anthroposophische Leitsätze, Der Erkenntnisweg der Anthroposophie—Das Michael-Mysterium* (volume 26 in the *Rudolf Steiner Gesamtausgabe* or Collected Works) published by Rudolf Steiner Verlag, Dornach. This authorized translation is published by kind permission of the Rudolf Steiner Nachlassverwaltung, Dornach

A catalogue record for this book is available from the British Library

ISBN 978 185584 096 6

Cover by Andrew Morgan
Typeset by DP Photosetting, Aylesbury, Bucks.
Printed and bound in Great Britain by 4edge Limited

This volume contains translations of the so-called 'Leading Thoughts,' brief paragraphs dealing with Anthroposophy as a Path of Knowledge. They were written by Rudolf Steiner for Members of the Anthroposophical Society and at a later stage were accompanied by communications known as the 'Letters' connected with sets of 'Leading Thoughts.' Articles with contents of a quite different kind, dealing with the character, aims and problems of the Society, are published separately, in two volumes entitled *The Life, Nature and Cultivation of Anthroposophy* and *The Constitution of the School of Spiritual Science.*

The 'Leading Thoughts' are printed here in the order in which they first appeared in German and are numbered consecutively from 1 to 185, to facilitate reference. The translations of the Leading Thoughts and of accompanying 'Letters' are those that were printed in the periodical *Anthroposophical Movement* during 1924 and the early months of 1925 until publication came to an end with Rudolf Steiner's death. The later Letters and Leading Thoughts (from No. 79 to the end) formed a continuous series and until now have been available as a separate volume, the last edition of which was entitled *The Michael Mystery*, translated by Mrs. E. Bowen Wedgwood. As, however, the original translations of all the Leading Thoughts and of nearly all the Letters accompanying them were the work of George and Mary Adams, they have been used throughout the present volume for the sake of uniformity of language and literary style.

CONTENTS

The titles given by Rudolf Steiner to his *Letters to Members* are shown in italics. The related dates were appended by him at the time of writing. The titles in plain type for the *Leading Thoughts* are added in this edition for the convenience of students, and the dates refer to the issue of the members' news sheet *'Was in der Anthroposophischen Gesellschaft vorgeht'* in which they were first published. The various numbering systems are given for the convenience of Groups working also with earlier editions.

In future there will be found in these columns something in the nature of anthroposophical 'Leading Thoughts' or principles. These may be taken to contain advice on the direction which members can give to the lectures and discussions in the several Groups. It is but a stimulus and suggestion which the Goetheanum would like to give to the whole Society. The independence of individual leading members in their work is in no way to be interfered with. We shall develop healthily if the Society gives free play to what leading members have to offer in all the different Groups. This will enrich and make manifold the life of the Society.

But it should also be possible for a unity of consciousness to arise in the whole Society—which will happen if the initiative and ideas that emerge at different places become known everywhere. Thus in these columns we shall sum up in short paragraphs the descriptions and lines of thought given by me in my lectures to the Society at the Goetheanum. I imagine that those who lecture or conduct the discussions in the Groups will be able to take what is here given as guiding lines, with which they may freely connect what they have to say. This will contribute to the unity and organic wholeness of the work of the Society without there being any question of constraint.

The plan will become fruitful for the whole Society if it meets with a true response—if the leading members will inform the Executive at the Goetheanum too of the content and nature of their own lectures and suggestions. Then only shall we grow, from a chaos of separate Groups, into a Society with a real spiritual content.

The Leading Thoughts here given are meant to open up subjects for study and discussion. Points of contact with them will be found in countless places in the anthroposophical books and lecture-courses, so that the subjects thus opened up can be enlarged upon and the discussions in the Groups centred around them.

When new ideas emerge among leading members in the several Groups, these too can be brought into connection with the suggestions we shall send out from the Goetheanum. We would thus provide an open framework for all the spiritual activity in the Society.

Spiritual activity can of course only thrive by free unfoldment on the part of the active individuals—and we must never sin against this truth. But there is no need to do so when one group or member within the Society acts in proper harmony with the other. If such co-operation were impossible, the attachment of individuals or groups to the Society would always remain a purely external thing—where it should in fact be felt as an *inner* reality.

It cannot be allowed that the existence of the Anthroposophical Society is merely made use of by this or that individual as an opportunity to say what he personally wishes to say with this or that intention. The Society must rather be the place where true *Anthroposophy* is cultivated. Anything that is *not* Anthroposophy can, after all, be pursued outside it. The Society is not there for extraneous objects.

It has not helped us that in the last few years individual members have brought into the Society their own personal wishes simply because they thought that as it increased it would become a suitable sphere of action for them. It may be said, Why was this not met and counteracted with the proper firmness? If that had been done, we should now be hearing it said on all sides, 'Oh, if only the initiative that arose in this or that quarter had been followed up at the time, how much farther we should be to-day!' Well, many things were followed up, which ended in sad disaster and only resulted in throwing us back.

But now it is enough. The demonstrations which individual experimenters in the Society wished to provide are done with. Such things need not be repeated endlessly. In the Executive at the Goetheanum we have a body which intends to cultivate Anthroposophy itself; and the Society should be an association of human beings who have the same object and are ready to enter into a living understanding with the Executive in the pursuit of it.

We must not think that our ideal in the Society can be attained from one day to the next. Time will be needed, and patience too. If we imagined that what lay in the intentions of the Christmas meeting could be brought into existence in a few weeks' time, this again would be harmful.

Anthroposophical Leading Thoughts given out as suggestions from the Goetheanum

1. Anthroposophy is a path of knowledge, to guide the Spiritual in the human being to the Spiritual in the universe. It arises in man as a need of the heart, of the life of feeling; and it can be justified only inasmuch as it can satisfy this inner need. He alone can acknowledge Anthroposophy, who finds in it what he himself in his own inner life feels impelled to seek. Hence only they can be anthroposophists who feel certain questions on the nature of man and the universe as an elemental need of life, just as one feels hunger and thirst.

2. Anthroposophy communicates knowledge that is gained in a spiritual way. Yet it only does so because everyday life, and the science founded on sense-perception and intellectual activity, lead to a barrier along life's way—a limit where the life of the soul in man would die if it could go no farther. Everyday life and science do not lead to this limit in such a way as to compel man to stop short at it. For at the very frontier where the knowledge derived from sense-perception ceases, there is opened through the human soul itself the further outlook into the spiritual world.

3. There are those who believe that with the limits of knowledge derived from sense-perception the limits of all insight are given. Yet if they would carefully observe *how* they become conscious of these limits, they would find in the very consciousness of the limits the faculties to transcend them. The fish swims up to the limits of the water; it must return because it lacks the physical organs to live outside this element. Man reaches the limits of knowledge attainable by sense-perception; but he can recognise that on the way to this point powers of soul have arisen in him—powers whereby the soul can live in an element that goes beyond the horizon of the senses.

Further Leading Thoughts issued from the Goetheanum for the Anthroposophical Society

4. For certainty of feeling and for a strong unfolding of his will, man needs a knowledge of the spiritual world. However widely he may feel the greatness, beauty and wisdom of the natural world, this world gives him no answer to the question of his own being. His own being holds together the materials and forces of the natural world in the living and sensitive form of man until the moment when he passes thıough the gate of death. Then Nature receives this human form, and Nature cannot hold it together; she can but dissolve and disperse it. Great, beautiful, widsom-filled Nature does indeed answer the question, How is the human form dissolved and destroyed? but not the other question, How is it maintained and held together? No theoretical objection can dispel this question from the feeling soul of man, unless indeed he prefers to lull himself to sleep. The presence of this question must incessantly maintain alive, in every human soul that is really awake, the longing for spiritual paths of World-knowledge.

5. For peace in his inner life, man needs Self-knowledge in the Spirit. He finds himself in his Thinking, Feeling and Willing. He sees how Thinking, Feeling and Willing are dependent on the natural man. In all their developments, they must follow the health and sickness, the strengthening and weakening of the body. Every sleep blots them out. Thus the experience of everyday life shows the spiritual consciousness of man in the greatest imaginable dependence on his bodily existence. Man suddenly becomes aware that in this realm of ordinary experience Self-knowledge may be utterly lost—the search for it a vain quest. Then first the anxious question arises: Can there be a Self-knowledge transcending the ordinary experiences of life? Can we have any certainty at all, as to a true Self of man? Anthroposophy would fain answer this question on a firm basis of spiritual experience. In so doing it takes its stand, not on any opinion or belief, but on a conscious experience in the Spirit—an experience in its own nature no less certain than the conscious experience in the body.

Further Leading Thoughts issued from the Goetheanum for the Anthroposophical Society

6. When we look out on lifeless Nature, we find a world full of inner relationships of law and order. We seek for these relationships and find in them the content of the 'Laws of Nature.' We find, moreover, that by virtue of these Laws lifeless Nature forms a connected whole with the entire Earth. We may now pass from this earthly connection which rules in all lifeless things, to contemplate the living world of plants. We see how the Universe beyond the Earth sends in from distances of space the forces which draw the Living forth out of the womb of the Lifeless. In all living things we are made aware of an element of being, which, freeing itself from the mere earthly connection, makes manifest the

forces that work down on to the Earth from realms of cosmic space. As in the eye we become aware of the luminous object which confronts it, so in the tiniest plant we are made aware of the nature of the Light from beyond the Earth. Through this ascent in contemplation, we can perceive the difference of the earthly and physical which holds sway in the lifeless world, from the extra-earthly and ethereal which abounds in all living things.

7. We find man with his transcendent being of soul and spirit placed into this world of the earthly and the extra-earthly. Inasmuch as he is placed into the earthly connection which contains all lifeless things, he bears with him his physical body. Inasmuch as he unfolds within him the forces which the living world draws into this earthly sphere from cosmic space, he has an etheric or life-body. The trend of science in modern times has taken no account of this essential contrast of the earthly and the ethereal. For this very reason, science has given birth to the most impossible conceptions of the ether. For fear of losing their way in fanciful and nebulous ideas, scientists have refrained from dwelling on the real contrast. But unless we do so, we can attain no true insight into the Universe and Man.

Further Leading Thoughts issued from the Goetheanum for the Anthroposophical Society

8. We may consider the nature of man in so far as it results from his physical and his etheric body. We shall find that all the phenomena of man's life which proceed from this side of his nature remain in the unconscious, nor do they ever lead to consciousness. Consciousness is not lighted up but darkened when the activity of the physical and the etheric body is enhanced. Conditions of faintness and the like can be recognised as the result of such enhancement. Following up this

line of thought, we recognise that something is at work in man—and in the animal—which is *not* of the same nature as the physical and the etheric. It takes effect, not when the forces of the physical and the etheric are active in their own way, but when they cease to be thus active. In this way we arrive at the conception of the astral body.

9. The *reality* of this astral body is discovered when we rise in meditation from the Thinking that is stimulated by the outer senses to an inner act of Vision. To this end, the Thinking that is stimulated from without must be taken hold of inwardly, and experienced as such, intensely in the soul, apart from its relation to the outer world. Through the strength of soul thus engendered, we become aware that there are inner organs of perception, which see a spiritual reality working in the animal and man at the very point where the physical and the etheric body are held in check in order that consciousness may arise.

10. Consciousness, therefore, does not arise by a further enhancement of activities which proceed from the physical and etheric bodies. On the contrary, these two bodies, with their activities, must be reduced to zero—nay even below zero—to 'make room' for the working of consciousness. They do not generate consciousness, they only furnish the ground on which the Spirit must stand in order to bring forth consciousness within the earthly life. As man on Earth needs the ground on which to stand, so does the Spiritual, within the earthly realm, need a material foundation on which it may unfold itself. And as a planet in the cosmic spaces does not require any ground beneath it in order to assert its place, so too the Spirit, when it looks—not through the senses into material—but through its own power into spiritual things, needs no material foundation to call its conscious activity to life.

Further Leading Thoughts issued from the Goetheanum for the Anthroposophical Society

11. The Self-consciousness which is summed up in the 'I' or 'Ego' emerges out of the sea of consciousness. Consciousness arises when the forces of the physical and etheric bodies disintegrate these bodies, and thus make way for the Spiritual to enter into man. For through this disintegration is provided the ground on which the life of consciousness can develop. If, however, the organism is not to be destroyed, the disintegration must be followed by a reconstruction. Thus, when for an experience in consciousness a process of disintegration has taken place, that which has been demolished will be built up again exactly. The experience of Self-consciousness lies in the perception of this upbuilding process. The same process can be observed with inner vision. We then feel how the Conscious is led over into the Self-conscious by man's *creating out of himself* an after-image of the merely Conscious. The latter has its image in the emptiness, as it were, produced within the organism by the disintegration. It has passed into Self-consciousness when the emptiness has been filled up again from within. The Being, capable of this 'fulfilment,' is experienced as 'I.'

12. The reality of the 'I' is found when the inner vision whereby the astral body is known and taken hold of, is carried a stage further. The Thinking which has become alive in meditation must now be permeated by the Will. To begin with we simply gave ourselves up to this new Thinking, without active Will. We thereby enabled spiritual realities to enter into this thinking life, even as in outer sense-perception colour enters the eye or sound the ear. What we have thus called to life in our consciousness by a more passive devotion, must now be reproduced by ourselves, by an act of Will. When we do so, there enters into this act of Will the perception of our own 'I' or Ego.

13. On the path of meditation we discover, beside the form in which the 'I' occurs in ordinary consciousness, three further forms: (1) In the consciousness which takes hold of the etheric body, the 'I' appears in picture-form; yet the picture is at the same time active Being, and as such it gives man form and figure, growth, and the plastic forces that create his body. (2) In the consciousness which takes hold of the astral body, the 'I' is manifested as a member of a spiritual world whence it receives its forces. (3) In the consciousness just indicated, as the last to be achieved, the 'I' reveals itself as a self-contained spiritual Being—relatively independent of the surrounding spiritual world.

Further Leading Thoughts issued from the Goetheanum for the Anthroposophical Society

14. The second form of the 'I'—first of the three forms that were indicated in the last section—appears as a 'picture' of the I. When we become aware of this picture-character, a light is also thrown on the quality of thought in which the 'I' appears before the ordinary consciousness. With all manner of reflections, men have sought within this consciousness for the 'true I.' Yet an earnest insight into the experiences of the ordinary consciousness will suffice to show that the 'true I' cannot be found therein. Only a shadow-in-thought is able to appear there—a shadowy reflection, even less than a picture. The truth of this seizes us all the more when we progress to the 'I' as a picture, which lives in the etheric body. Only now are we rightly kindled to *search* for the 'I', for the true being of man.

15. Insight into the form in which the 'I' lives in the astral body leads to a right feeling of the relation of man to the spiritual world. For ordinary consciousness this form of the 'I' is buried in the dark depths of the unconscious, where

man enters into connection with the spiritual being of the Universe through Inspiration. Ordinary consciousness experiences only a faint echo-in-feeling of this Inspiration from the wide expanse of the spiritual world, which holds sway in depths of the soul.

16. It is the third form of the 'I' which gives us insight into the independent Being of man within a spiritual world. It makes us feel how, with his earthly-sensible nature, man stands before himself as a mere manifestation of what he really is. Here lies the starting-point of true Self-knowledge. For the Self which fashions man in his true nature is revealed to him in Knowledge only when he progresses from the thought of the 'I' to its picture, from the picture to the creative forces of the picture, and from the creative forces to the spiritual Beings who sustain them.

Further Leading Thoughts issued from the Goetheanum for the Anthroposophical Society

17. Man is a being who unfolds his life in the midst, between two regions of the world. With his bodily development he is a member of a 'lower world'; with his soul-nature he himself constitutes a 'middle world'; and with his faculties of Spirit he is ever striving towards an 'upper world.' He owes his bodily development to all that Nature has given him; he bears the being of his soul within him as his own portion; and he discovers in himself the forces of the Spirit, as the gifts that lead him out beyond himself to participate in a Divine World.

18. The Spirit is creative in these three regions of the World. Nature is not void of Spirit. We lose even Nature from our knowledge if we do not become aware of the Spirit within her. Nevertheless, in Nature's existence we find the Spirit as it were asleep. Yet just as sleep has its task in human life—as

the 'I' must be asleep at one time in order to be the more awake at another—so must the World-Spirit be asleep where Nature is, in order to be the more awake elsewhere.

19. In relation to the World, the soul of man is like a dreamer if it does not pay heed to the Spirit at work within it. The Spirit awakens the dreams of the soul from their ceaseless weaving in the inner life, to active participation in the World where man's true Being has its origin. As the dreamer shuts himself off from the surrounding physical world and entwines himself into himself, so would the soul lose connection with the Spirit of the World in whom it has its source, if it turned a deaf ear to the awakening calls of the Spirit within it.

Further Leading Thoughts issued from the Goetheanum for the Anthroposophical Society

20. For a right development of the life of the human soul, it is essential for man to become fully conscious of working actively from out of spiritual sources in his being. Many adherents of the modern scientific world-conception are victims of a strong prejudice in this respect. They say that a universal causality is dominant in all phenomena of the world; and that if man believes that he himself, out of his own resources, can be the cause of anything, it is a mere illusion on his part. Modern Natural Science wishes to follow observation and experience faithfully in all things, but in its prejudice about the hidden causality of man's inner sources of action it sins against its own principle. For the free and active working, straight from the inner resources of the human being, is a perfectly elementary experience of self-observation. It cannot be argued away; rather must we harmonise it with our insight into the universal causation of things within the order of Nature.

21. Non-recognition of this impulse out of the Spirit working in the inner life of man, is the greatest hindrance to the attainment of an insight into the spiritual world. For to consider our own being as a mere part of the order of Nature is in reality to divert the soul's attention from our own being. Nor can we penetrate into the spiritual world unless we first take hold of the Spirit where it is immediately given to us, namely in clear and open-minded self-observation.

22. Self-observation is the first beginning in the observation of the Spirit. It can indeed be the right beginning, for if it is true, man cannot possibly stop short at it, but is bound to progress to the further spiritual content of the World. As the human body pines away when bereft of physical nourishment, so will the man who rightly observes himself feel that his Self is becoming stunted if he does not see working into it the forces from a creative spiritual World outside him.

Further Leading Thoughts issued from the Goetheanum for the Anthroposophical Society

23. Passing through the gate of death, man goes out into the spiritual world, in that he feels falling away from him all the impressions and contents of soul which he received during earthly life through the bodily senses and the brain. His consciousness then has before it in an all-embracing picture-tableau the whole content of life which, during his earthly wanderings, entered as pictureless thoughts into his memory, or which—remaining unnoticed by the earthly consciousness—nevertheless made a subconscious impression on his soul. After a very few days these pictures grow faint and fade away. When they have altogether vanished, he knows that he has laid aside his etheric body too; for in the etheric body he can recognise the bearer of these pictures.

24. Having laid aside the etheric body, man has the astral body and the Ego as the members of his being still remaining to him. The astral body, so long as it is with him, brings to his consciousness all that during earthly life was the unconscious content of the soul when at rest in sleep. This content includes the judgments instilled into the astral body by Spirit-beings of a higher World during the periods of sleep—judgments which remain concealed from earthly consciousness. Man now lives through his earthly life a second time, yet so, that the content of his soul is now the judgment of his thought and action from the standpoint of the Spirit-world. He lives it through in backward order: first the last night, then the last but one, and so on.

25. This judgment of his life, which man experiences in the astral body after passing through the gate of death, lasts as long as the sum-total of the times he spent during his earthly life in sleep.

Further Leading Thoughts issued from the Goetheanum for the Anthroposophical Society

26. Only when the astral body has been laid aside—when the judgment of his life is over—man enters the spiritual world. There he stands in like relation to Beings of purely spiritual character as on Earth to the beings and processes of the Nature-kingdoms. In spiritual experience, everything that was his outer world on Earth now becomes his inner world. He no longer merely perceives it, but experiences it in its spiritual being which was hid from him on Earth, as his own world.

27. In the Spirit-realm, man as he is on Earth becomes an outer world. We gaze upon him, even as on Earth we gaze upon the stars and clouds, the mountains and rivers. Nor is

this 'outer world' any less rich in content than the glory of the Cosmos as it appears to us in earthly life.

28. The forces begotten by the human Spirit in the Spirit-realm work on in the fashioning of earthly Man, even as the deeds we accomplish in the Physical work on as a content of the soul in the life after death.

Further Leading Thoughts issued from the Goetheanum for the Anthroposophical Society

29. In the evolved Imaginative Knowledge there works what lives as soul and spirit in the inner life of man, fashioning the physical body in its life, and unfolding man's existence in the physical world on this bodily foundation. Over against the physical body, whose substances are renewed again and again in the process of metabolism, we here come to the inner nature of man, unfolding itself *continuously* from birth (or conception) until death. Over against the physical Space-body, we come to a Time-body.

30. In the Inspired Knowledge there lives, in picture-form, what man experiences in a spiritual environment in the time between death and a new birth. What Man is in his own Being and in relation to cosmic worlds—without the physical and etheric bodies by means of which he undergoes his earthly life—is here made visible.

31. In the Intuitive Knowledge there comes to consciousness the working-over of former earthly lives into the present. In the further course of evolution these former lives have been divested of their erstwhile connections with the physical world. They have become the purely spiritual kernel of man's being, and, as such, are working in his present life. In this way, they too are an object of Knowledge—of that

Knowledge which results with the further unfolding of the Imaginative and Inspired.

Further Leading Thoughts issued from the Goetheanum for the Anthroposophical Society

32. In the head of man, the physical organisation is a copy, an impress of the spiritual individuality. The physical and the etheric part of the head stand out as complete and self-contained pictures of the Spiritual; *beside* them, in independent soul-spiritual existence, there stand the astral and the Ego-part. Thus in the head of man we have to do with a development, side by side, of the physical and etheric, relatively independent on the one hand, and of the astral and Ego-organisation on the other.

33. In the limbs- and metabolic part of man the four members of the human being are intimately bound up with one another. The Ego-organisation and astral body are not there *beside* the physical and etheric part. They are *within* them, vitalising them, working in their growth, their faculty of movement and so forth. Through this very fact, the limbs- and metabolic part of man is like a germinating seed, striving for ever to unfold; striving continually to become a 'head,' and—during the earthly life of man—no less continually prevented.

34. The rhythmic organisation stands in the midst. Here the Ego-organisation and astral body alternately unite with the physical and etheric part, and loose themselves again. The breathing and the circulation of the blood are the physical impress of this alternate union and loosening. The in-breathing process portrays the union; the outbreathing the loosening. The processes in the arterial blood represent the union; those in the venous blood the loosening.

Further Leading Thoughts issued from the Goetheanum for the Anthroposophical Society

35. We understand the physical nature of man only if we regard it as a *picture* of the soul and spirit. Taken by itself, the physical corporality of man is unintelligible. But it is a picture of the soul and spirit in different ways in its several members. The head is the most perfect and complete symbolic picture of the soul and spirit. All that pertains to the system of the metabolism and the limbs is like a picture that has not yet assumed its finished forms, but is still being worked upon. Lastly, in all that belongs to the rhythmic organisation of man, the relation of the soul and spirit to the body is intermediate between these opposites.

36. If we contemplate the human head from this spiritual point of view, we shall find in it a help to the understanding of spiritual Imaginations. For in the forms of the head, Imaginative forms are as it were coagulated to the point of physical density.

37. Similarly, if we contemplate the rhythmic part of man's organisation it will help us to understand Inspirations. The physical appearance of the rhythms of life bears even in the sense-perceptible picture the character of Inspiration. Lastly, in the system of the metabolism and the limbs—if we observe it in full action, in the exercise of its necessary or possible functions—we have a picture, supersensible yet sensible, of pure supersensible Intuitions.

ON THE PICTURE-NATURE OF MAN

Supplementary to the last set of Leading Thoughts

It is most important that it should be understood through Anthroposophy that the ideas which a man gains by looking at outer Nature are inadequate for the observation of Man. The ideas which have taken possession of men's minds during the spiritual development of the last few centuries fail to realise this fact. Through them men have grown accustomed to thinking out natural laws, and to explaining by means of them the phenomena which are perceived by the senses. They then turn their attention to the human organism, and think that that too can be explained through bringing the laws of Nature to bear upon it.

Now this is just as though, in considering a picture which a painter had created, we only took into account the substance of the colours, their power of adhering to the canvas, the way in which these colours were applied, and similar things. But such a way of regarding the picture does not reveal what is contained in it. Quite other laws are active in the revelation contained in the picture than those which can be perceived by considering such points as these.

It is a question of realising that in the human being too something is revealed which cannot be grasped from the standpoint of natural law. If anyone has once thoroughly made this conception his own, then he will be able to understand man *as a picture*. A mineral is not a picture in this sense. It reveals only what is directly evident to the senses.

To a certain extent when regarding a picture we look *through* what the senses perceive to its spiritual content. And so is it also in the observation of the human being. If we truly understand the human being in the light of natural law, we do not feel that these laws bring us into contact with the real man, but only with that through which he reveals himself.

We must experience spiritually that when we regard a man only from the point of view of natural law, it is as if we stood before a picture seeing only 'blue' and 'red,' and quite unable through an inner activity of the soul to relate the blue and red to that which reveals itself through these colours.

When viewing things from the standpoint of natural law we must perceive the mineral in one way, the human being in another. In the case of the mineral it is, for the spiritual understanding, as if we were in immediate touch with what is perceived; but in the case of man it is as though we could only come as near to him through natural laws as to a picture which we do not see clearly with the eye of the soul but only touch and feel.

When once we have gained the perception that man is a 'picture' of something, we shall be in the right mood of soul to progress to that which manifests in this picture.

The pictorial nature of man does not manifest in one way only. An organ of sense is in its nature least of all a picture, and mostly a kind of manifestation of itself like the mineral. The human organs of sense approach nearest to natural laws. Let us but contemplate the wonderful arrangement of the eye, which by natural laws we are able to comprehend. It is the same with the other organs, though not often so clearly evident. It is because the sense organs, in their formation, show a certain compactness. They are arranged in the organism as complete formations, and as such assist in the perception of the outer world.

But it is otherwise with the rhythmic actions in the organism. They are not complete, but evanescent, the organism in them continually forming and then declining. If the sense organs were like the rhythmic system, we should perceive the outer world in a perpetual growth.

The sense organs are like a picture on the wall. The rhythmic system is like the scene that unfolds itself if canvas and painter are imaged by us at the conception of the picture. The picture is not yet there, but it comes more and more into being. In studying the rhythmic system, we have to do with a perpetual process of becoming. A thing that has already come into existence remains in existence, for a time at any rate. But when we study the human rhythmic system we find the process of becoming, the upbuilding process, followed directly and without a gap by the passing out of existence, the destructive process. In the rhythmic system there manifests itself a picture, coming into existence, but never finished nor complete.

The activity which the soul discharges in conscious devotion to what is brought before it as the finished picture, may be styled *Imagination*. On the other hand *Inspiration* is the experience that must be unfolded in order to comprehend a growing picture.

But this is different again in the contemplation of the metabolic and limb system. Here it is as if one was before a bare canvas and unused paints, and an artist not even painting. To get a perception of the metabolic and limb system, one must get a perception that has as little connection with the senses, as have the bare canvas and unused paints with that which is afterwards the artist's picture. And the activity that is developed by the soul in pure spirituality out of the metabolic and limb system is as when, upon seeing the painter and an empty canvas and unused paints, one experiences the picture to be painted later. In order to understand the metabolic and limb system the soul must exercise the power of *Intuition.*

It is necessary that the active members of the Anthroposophical Society should concentrate in this way on the essential and fundamental nature of anthroposophical study. For it is not only the knowledge one gains by study but the experience achieved thereby that matters.

From what has here been explained our study will lead us to the following Leading Thoughts.

Further Leading Thoughts issued from the Goetheanum for the Anthroposophical Society

38. We have shown how man is to be regarded in his picture-nature and in the spirituality which thereby reveals itself. Once this perception is attained, then, in the spiritual world where we see man living and moving as a Spirit-being, we are also on the point of seeing the reality of the moral laws of the soul. For the moral world-order is then revealed as the earthly image of an order belonging to the spiritual world. The physical world-order and the moral are welded together now, in undivided unity.

39. From out of man, there works the human Will. This Will confronts the 'Laws of Nature' which we derive from the external world, as something altogether foreign to their essence. The nature of the sense-organs can still be scientifically understood by virtue of their likeness to the objects of external Nature. In the activity of these organs, the Will, however, is not yet able to unfold itself. The nature that manifests itself in the human rhythmic system is already far less like any external thing. Into this system the Will can already work to some extent. But the rhythmic system is in constant process of coming-into-being and passing-away, and in these processes the Will is not yet free.

40. In the system of metabolism and the limbs we have a nature which manifests itself in material substances and in the processes they undergo; yet are the substances and processes in reality no nearer to this nature than are the artist and his materials to the finished picture. Here, therefore, the Will is able to enter in and work directly. Behind the human organisation living in 'Natural Laws,' we must grasp that inner human nature which lives and moves and has its being in the Spiritual. Here is the realm in which we can become aware of the real working of the Will. For the realm of

sense, the human Will remains a mere word, empty of all content, and the scientist or thinker who claims to take hold of it within this realm, leaves the real nature of the Will behind him and replaces it in theory by something else.

Further Leading Thoughts issued from the Goetheanum for the Anthroposophical Society

41. In the third of the last Leading Thoughts, we pointed to the nature of the human Will. Only when this is realised, do we enter with understanding into a sphere of the world where Destiny or Karma works. So long as we perceive only that system of law which holds sway in the relations of the things and facts of Nature, our understanding is entirely remote from the laws that work in Destiny.

42. When the law in Destiny is thus perceived, it is revealed at the same time that Destiny cannot come into existence in the course of a single physical life on Earth. So long as he inhabits the same physical body, man can realise only the moral content of his Will in the way that this particular physical body, within the physical world, allows. Only when he has passed through the gate of death into the sphere of the Spirit, can the Spirit-nature of the Will come to full effect. Then will the Good and the Evil be severally realised—a spiritual realisation to begin with—in their corresponding outcome.

43. In this spiritual realisation man fashions and forms himself between death and a new birth. He becomes *in being* an image of what he *did* during his earthly life; and out of this his being, on his subsequent return to Earth, he forms his physical life. The Spiritual that works and weaves in Destiny can only find realisation in the Physical if its corresponding cause withdrew, before this realisation, into the spiritual

realm. For all that emerges in our life by way of Destiny proceeds *out of the Spiritual*; nor does it ever take shape within the sequence of physical phenomena.

Further Leading Thoughts issued from the Goetheanum for the Anthroposophical Society

44. We should pass on to a spiritual-scientific treatment of the question of Destiny by taking examples from the life and experience of individual men and women, showing how the forces of Destiny work themselves out, and the significance they have for the whole course of human life. We may show, for instance, how an experience which a man undergoes in his youth, which he can certainly not have brought upon himself entirely of his own free will, may none the less to a large extent give shape to the whole of his later life.

45. We should describe the significance of the fact that in the physical course of life between birth and death the good may become unhappy in their outer life, and the wicked at any rate apparently happy. In expounding these things, pictures of individual cases carry more weight than theoretical explanations; they are a far better preparation for the spiritual-scientific treatment of the subject.

46. Events of Destiny which come into the life of man in such a way that their determining conditions cannot possibly be found in his present life, should be cited. Faced with such happenings, a purely reasonable view of life already points in the direction of former lives on Earth. It must of course be made clear by the very way in which these things are described that no dogmatic or binding statement is implied. The purpose of such examples is simply to direct one's thoughts towards a spiritual-scientific treatment of the question of Destiny.

Further Leading Thoughts issued from the Goethaenum for the Anthroposophical Society

47. Of all that is latent in the forming of man's Destiny, only the very smallest part enters the everyday consciousness. Yet the unveiling of our Destiny teaches us most of all, how the Unconscious can indeed be brought to consciousness. They in effect are wrong, who speak of what is, for the time being, the Unconscious, as though it must remain absolutely in the realm of the unknown, thus constituting a barrier of knowledge. With every fragment of his Destiny that is unveiled to him, man lifts into the realm of consciousness something that was hitherto unconscious.

48. In so doing man becomes aware that the things of Destiny are not woven within the life between birth and death. Thus the question of Destiny impels him most of all to the contemplation of the life between death and a new birth.

49. Conscious human experience is thus impelled by the question of Destiny to look beyond itself. Moreover, as we dwell upon this fact, we shall develop a true feeling for the relation of the Natural and the Spiritual. He who beholds the living sway of Destiny in the human being, stands already in the midst of spiritual things. For the inner connections of Destiny have nothing of the character of outer Nature.

Further Leading Thoughts issued from the Goetheanum for the Anthroposophical Society

50. It is most important to point out, how the study of the historic life of mankind is called to life when we show that it is the souls of men themselves, passing from epoch to epoch

in their repeated lives on Earth, who carry over the results of one historic age into another.

51. It may easily be objected that such a line of thought robs history of its naïve and elemental force. But this objection is untrue. On the contrary, our vision of historic life is deepened when we can trace it thus into man's inmost being. History becomes more real and more abundant, not poorer and more abstract. In describing these things we must, however, unfold true sympathy and insight into the living soul of man, for we gaze deep into the soul along these lines of thought.

52. The epochs in the life between death and a new birth should be treated in relation to the forming of Karma. Further Leading Thoughts will indicate the way in which this can be done.

Further Leading Thoughts issued from the Goetheanum for the Anthroposophical Society

53. The unfolding of man's life between death and a new birth takes place in successive stages. For a few days after passing through the gate of Death the whole of the past earthly life is seen in living *pictures*. This experience reveals at the same time the gradual severance of the vehicle of the past life from the human soul-and-spirit.

54. In a time that comprises about a third of the past earthly life, the soul discovers in spiritual experiences the effect which this life must have in accordance with an ethically just World-order. During this experience the purpose is begotten in the soul to shape the next earthly life in a corresponding way, and thus to compensate for the past.

55. There follows a purely spiritual epoch of existence. During this epoch, which is of long duration, the soul of man—along with other human souls karmically connected with him, and with the Beings of the Hierarchies above—fashions the next life on Earth in the sense of Karma.

Further Leading Thoughts issued from the Goetheanum for the Anthroposophical Society

56. The epoch of existence between death and a new birth, when the Karma of man is fashioned, can be described only by the results of spiritual research. But it must always be borne in mind that such description appeals to our intelligence. We need only consider with open mind the realities of the world of the senses, and we become aware that it points to a spiritual reality—as the form of a corpse points to the life that indwelt it.

57. The results of Spiritual Science show that between death and birth man belongs to Spirit-kingdoms, even as he belongs between birth and death to the three kingdoms of Nature: the mineral, the plant and the animal.

58. The mineral kingdom is recognisable in the form of the human being at any given moment; the plant kingdom, as the etheric body, is the basis of his growth, his becoming; the animal kingdom, as the astral body, is the impulse for his unfolding of sensation and volition. The crowning of the conscious life of sensation and volition in the *self-conscious* spiritual life makes the connection of man with the spiritual world straightway apparent.

Further Leading Thoughts issued from the Goetheanum for the Anthroposophical Society

59. Open-minded contemplation of Thinking shows that the thoughts of the ordinary consciousness have no existence of their own, but arise only as the reflected images of something. Man, however, feels himself to be alive in his thoughts. The thoughts are not alive, but he himself is living *in* them. This life has its source in Spirit-beings, whom we may describe (in the sense of my book, *Occult Science*) as the Beings of the Third Hierarchy—a kingdom of the Spirit.

60. Extended to the life of Feeling, the same open-minded contemplation shows that the feelings, though they arise out of the body, cannot have been created by it. For their life bears in it a character independent of the bodily organism. With his bodily nature man can feel himself to be within the world of Nature. Yet just in realising this with true self-understanding, he will feel that with his world of Feeling he is in a spiritual kingdom. This is the kingdom of the Second Hierarchy.

61. As a being of Will, man's attention is directed not to his own bodily nature, but to the outer world. When he desires to walk he does not ask, 'What do I feel in my feet?' but 'What is the goal out there, which I desire to reach?' In willing, man forgets his body. In his Will he belongs, not to his own nature, but to the Spirit-kingdom of the First Hierarchy.

UNDERSTANDING OF THE SPIRIT; CONSCIOUS EXPERIENCE OF DESTINY

This week something will be given in the communications addressed to members in these columns, which may serve to bring us to a further understanding of the weekly 'Leading Thoughts.'

The understanding of anthroposophical truth can be furthered if the relation which exists between man and the world is constantly brought before the human soul.

When man turns his attention to the world into which he is born and out of which he dies, he is surrounded in the first place by the fullness of his sense-impressions. He forms thoughts about these sense-impressions.

In bringing the following to his consciousness: 'I am forming thoughts about what my senses reveal to me as the world,' he has already come to the point where he can contemplate himself. He can say to himself: In my thoughts 'I' live. The world gives me the opportunity of experiencing *myself* in thoughts. I find myself in my thoughts when I contemplate the world.

And continuing to reflect in this way, he ceases to be conscious of the world; he becomes conscious of the 'I'. He ceases to have the world before him; he begins to experience the self.

If the experience be reversed, and the attention directed to the inner life in which the world is mirrored, then those events emerge into consciousness which belong to our life's destiny, and in which our human self has flowed along from the point of time to which our memory goes back. In following up the events of his destiny, a man experiences his own existence.

In bringing this to his consciousness: 'I with my own self have experienced something that destiny brought to me,' a man has already come to the point where he will contemplate the world. He can say to himself: I was not alone in my fate; the world played a part in my experience. I *willed* this or that; the world streamed into my will. I find the world in my will when I experience this will in self-contemplation.

Continuing thus to enter into his own being, man ceases to be conscious of the self, he becomes conscious of the world; he ceases to experience himself, he becomes feelingly aware of the world.

'I send my thoughts out into the World, there I find myself; I sink into myself, there I find the World.' If a man experiences this strongly enough he is confronted with the great riddles of the World and Man.

For to have the feeling: I have taken endless pains to understand the world through thinking, and after all there is but myself in this thinking—this gives rise to the first great riddle. And to feel that one's own self is formed through destiny, yet to perceive in this process the onward flow of world-happenings—this presents the second riddle.

In the experience of this problem of Man and the World germinates the frame of mind in which man can so confront Anthroposophy that he receives from it in his inner being an impression which rouses his attention.

For Anthroposophy asserts that there is a spiritual experience which does not lose the world when thinking. One can also *live* in thought. Anthroposophy tells of an inward experience in which one does not lose the sense-world when thinking, but gains the Spirit-world. Instead of penetrating into the ego in which the sense-world is felt to disappear, one penetrates into the Spirit-world in which the ego feels established.

Anthroposophy shows, further, that there is an experience of destiny in which one does not lose the self. In fate, too, one can still feel oneself to be active. Anthroposophy points out, in the impartial, unegoistic observation of human destiny, an experience in which one learns to love the world and not only one's own existence. Instead of staring into the world which carries the ego on the waves of fortune and misfortune, one finds the ego which shapes its own fate voluntarily. Instead of striking against the world on which the ego is dashed to pieces, one penetrates into the self, which feels itself united with the course of events in the world.

Man's destiny comes to him from the world that is revealed to him by his senses. If then he finds his own activity in the working of his destiny, his real self rises up before him not only out of his inner being but out of the sense-world too.

If a person is able to feel, however faintly, how the spiritual part of the world appears in the self, and how the self proves to be working in the outer world of sense, he has already learned to understand Anthroposophy correctly. For he will then realise that in Anthroposophy it is possible to describe the Spirit-world which the self can comprehend. And this will enable him to understand that in the sense-world the self can also be found—in a different way than by diving within. Anthroposophy finds the self by showing how the sense-world reveals to man not only sense-perceptions but also the after-effects of his life before birth and his former earthly lives.

Man can now gaze on the world perceptible to his senses and say: It contains not only colour, sound, warmth; in it are active the experiences passed through by souls before their present earthly life. And he can look into himself and say: I find there not only my ego but, in addition, a spiritual world is revealed.

In an understanding of this kind, a person who really feels—who is not unmoved by—the great riddles of Man and the World, can meet on a common ground with the Initiate who in accordance with his insight is obliged to speak of the outer world of the senses as manifesting not only sense-perceptions but also the impressions of what human souls have done in their life before birth and in past earthly lives, and who has to say of the world of the inner self that it reveals spiritual events which produce impressions and are as effective as the perceptions of the sense-world.

The would-be active members should consciously make themselves mediators between what the questioning human soul feels as the problems of Man and the Universe, and what the knowledge of the Initiates has to recount, when it draws forth a past world out of the destiny of human beings, and when by strengthening the soul it opens up the perception of a spiritual world.

In this way, through the work of the would-be active members, the Anthroposophical Society may become a true preparatory school for the school of Initiates. It was the intention of the Christmas Meeting to indicate this very forcibly; and one who truly understands what that Meeting meant will continue to point this out until sufficient understanding of it can bring the Society fresh tasks and possibilities again.

May the Leading Thoughts to be given in this number proceed, therefore, out of this spirit.

Further Leading Thoughts issued from the Goetheanum for the Anthroposophical Society

62. In our sense-perceptions, the world of the senses bears on to the surface only a portion of the being that lies concealed in the depths of its waves beneath. Penetrative spiritual observation reveals within these depths the after-effects of what was done by souls of men in ages long gone by.

63. To ordinary self-observation the inner world of man reveals only a portion of that, in the midst of which it stands. Intensified experience in consciousness shows it to be contained within a living spiritual Reality.

64. The destiny of man reveals the workings, not only of an external world, but of the man's own Self.

65. The experiences of the human soul reveal not only a Self but a world of the Spirit, which the Self can know by deeper spiritual knowledge as a world united with its own being.

Further Leading Thoughts issued from the Goetheanum for the Anthroposophical Society

66. The Beings of the Third Hierarchy reveal themselves in the life which is unfolded as a spiritual background in human Thinking. In the human activity of thought this life is concealed. If it worked on in its own essence in human thought, man could not attain to Freedom. Where cosmic Thought-activity ceases, human Thought-activity begins.

67. The Beings of the Second Hierarchy manifest themselves in a world-of-soul beyond humanity—a world of cosmic soul-activities, hidden from human Feeling. This cosmic world-of-soul is ever creative in the background of human Feeling. Out of the being of man it first creates the organism of Feeling; only then can it bring Feeling itself to life therein.

68. The Beings of the First Hierarchy manifest themselves in spiritual creation beyond humanity—a cosmic world of spiritual Being which indwells the human Willing. This world of cosmic Spirit experiences itself in creative action when man wills. It first creates the connection of man's being with the Universe beyond humanity; only then does man himself become, through his organism of Will, a freely willing being.

SPIRITUAL KINGDOMS AND HUMAN SELF-KNOWLEDGE

Through the Leading Thoughts which have been sent out from the Goetheanum during the past weeks to the members of the Anthroposophical Society, the soul has been directed to the Beings of the spiritual kingdoms with whom man is connected from above, just as, from below, he is connected with the kingdoms of Nature.

True self-knowledge may become the guide through which man finds his way into these spiritual kingdoms. And when such self-knowledge is striven after in the right way, then the understanding will be awakened for what Anthroposophy is able to make known through its insight into the life of the spiritual world. But self-knowledge must be practised in the true sense, not as a mere rigid gazing into one's inner being.

By means of such a true self-knowledge one arrives in the first place at what lives in *memory*. In thought-pictures, the shadow of what was a direct and living experience in the past is called up into consciousness. Anyone seeing a shadow will, out of an inner impulse of thought, be guided to the object which threw the shadow. He who bears a memory within him cannot in this direct way turn the eye of his soul to the experience which lives on in the memory. But when he truly reflects on his own nature he will be obliged to say to himself: that he himself, in his soul-being, is what his experiences have made of him—those experiences which throw their shadows into the memory. The memory-shadows appear in the consciousness; in the soul there *shines* what in the memory is *shadow*. Dead shadow lives in the memory; living being lives in the soul in which the memory is active.

It is only necessary that this relationship of the memory to the actual soul-life should be made clear; and in this striving for clearness in self-knowledge a man will then perceive that he is on the path to the spiritual world.

Through memory, man is looking at the spiritual in his own soul. But in the ordinary consciousness he does not arrive at a real grasp of what he thus looks upon. He looks in the direction on something; but his look meets with no reality. Anthroposophy, out of Imaginative Knowledge, shows the way to this reality. Through it we are referred from the shadow to that which gleams and shines. Anthroposophy does this, in that it speaks of the etheric body of man. It shows how the physical body is active in the thought-shadow pictures; but how in the gleaming and shining the etheric body *lives*.

With the physical body man is in the sense-world; with the etheric body he is in the etheric world. In the sense-world he has his environment; in the etheric world also. And Anthroposophy speaks of this latter environment as the first of the hidden worlds in which man is living. It is the kingdom of the Third Hierarchy.

Let us now approach *speech* in the same way that we have considered memory. It issues from within man just as does the memory. It connects him with a certain state of being, as memory unites him with his own experiences. In words, too, there is an element of shadow. This is deeper than the shadow of the thoughts of memory. When man inwardly casts the shadow of his experiences as his memories, his own hidden self is active in the whole process. He is there when the light casts the shadow.

In speech there is also a process of shadow-casting. The words are the shadows. What is it in this case that shines? Something stronger shines, because words are stronger shadows than are the thoughts of memory. The element in the human self which in the course of an earthly life can produce memories, cannot create words. Man must learn these in connection with other human beings. Something which lies deeper in him than that which casts the shadow of memory must take part in this process. In this case Anthroposophy speaks from Inspired Knowledge of the astral body, as in the case of memory it speaks of the etheric body. The astral body is added to the physical and etheric bodies as a third part of the human being.

This third part, too, has a cosmic environment about it. This is made up of the Second Hierarchy. In human language we have a phantom of this Second Hierarchy. As to his astral body, man lives within the province of this Hierarchy.

We may go still further. In speech a portion of man's being is engaged. When he speaks he brings his inner being into motion. That which surrounds this inner being remains at rest. The movement of speech wrings itself loose from the human being while he remains at rest, but the whole man comes into motion when he brings into activity all that belongs to his limbs. In such movement man is no less full of expression than in memory and speech. Memory expresses his experiences. The nature of language consists in its being the expression of something. In the same way the man whose whole being is in motion expresses something.

Anthroposophy points out that this 'something' is another part of the human being. From Intuitive Knowledge it speaks of the 'real Self' or 'I.' This too, it finds, has a cosmic environment, namely the First Hierarchy.

When man approaches the thoughts in his memory he meets with the first supersensible element—his own etheric being. Anthroposophy points out to him the cosmic environment corresponding to it. When man considers himself as one who makes use of language he finds his astral being. This is no longer comprehended in that which only acts inwardly, like memory. It is seen by Inspiration as that which in the act of speaking shapes a physical process out of the Spiritual. Speech is a physical process. At its foundation lies an activity which proceeds from the sphere of the Second Hierarchy.

When the whole man is in motion there is a more intense physical action than in speech. Not merely a part of man is moulded, the whole man is given shape; and in the physical being which lives and moves in form, the First Hierarchy is active.

In this way, then, true self-knowledge can be cultivated. But in doing this man does not grasp his own Self alone. Step by step he comprehends the parts of his body: the physical body, the etheric body, the astral body and the Self. And by comprehending these he also reaches up, step by step, to higher worlds which like the three kingdoms of Nature, the animal, plant and mineral kingdoms, belong, as the three spiritual kingdoms, to the whole Universe in which his being is unfolding.

Further Leading Thoughts issued from the Goetheanum for the Anthroposophical Society

69. The Third Hierarchy reveals itself as pure soul and spirit. It lives and moves in all that man experiences in the soul, in his inner life. Neither in the etheric nor in the physical could any processes arise if this Hierarchy alone were active. Soul-life alone could exist.

70. The Second Hierarchy reveals itself as soul and spirit that works in the etheric. All that is etheric is a manifestation of the Second Hierarchy. This Hierarchy, however, does not reveal itself directly in the physical; its power extends only to etheric processes. Only etheric and soul-life could exist if the Third and the Second Hierarchy alone were active.

71. The First and strongest Hierarchy reveals itself as the spiritually active principle within the physical. It makes the physical world into a Cosmos. The Third and the Second Hierarchy are the Beings who minister to it in this activity.

Further Leading Thoughts issued from the Goetheanum for the Anthroposophical Society

72. As soon as we approach the higher members of man's being—the etheric, the astral body and the Ego-organisation—we are obliged to seek for man's relation to the beings of the spiritual kingdoms. It is only the physical body's organisation which we can illumine by reference to the three physical kingdoms of Nature.

73. In the etheric body the Intelligence of the Cosmos becomes embodied in the human being. That this can happen, requires the activity of cosmic Beings, who, in their combined working, shape the etheric body of man, even as the physical forces shape the physical.

74. In the astral body the spiritual world implants the moral impulses into the human being. That these can show forth their life in man's organisation, depends on the activity of Beings who are able not only to think the Spiritual, but to shape it in its reality.

75. In the Ego-organisation man experiences himself, even in the physical body, as a Spirit. That this can happen, requires the activity of Beings who themselves, as spiritual Beings, live in the physical world.

Those who want to take an active part in the Movement may find in the Leading Thoughts that are given out from the Goetheanum, an impulse and stimulus that shall enable them to bring unity and wholeness into all anthroposophical activity.

They will find in them, as they receive them week by week, guidance for deepening their understanding of the material that is already at hand in the Lecture-Courses and for putting it forward in the Group meetings with a certain order and harmony.

It would without doubt be more desirable for the lectures given in Dornach to be carried at once in all directions to the individual Groups. But one has to remember what complicated technical arrangements such a course would necessitate. The Executive at the Goetheanum are making every possible effort in this direction, and still more will be done in the future. But we must reckon with the possibilities that exist. The aims that found expression at the Christmas Meeting will be realised. But we need time.

For the present those Groups that have members who visit the Goetheanum, hear the lectures there and can bring back the substance of them into the Group meetings, have an advantage. And Groups should recognise that the sending of members to the Goetheanum in this way is a very good thing to do. On the other hand, however, the work that has already been achieved within the Anthroposophical Society and that is embodied in the printed Courses and Lectures, should not be undervalued. If you take up these Courses and call to mind from the titles what is contained in this one and in that, and then turn to the Leading Thoughts, you will find that you meet with one thing in one Course, another in another, that explains the Leading Thoughts more fully. By reading together passages that are found separated in different Courses, you will discover the right points of view for expounding and elaborating the Leading Thoughts.

We in the Anthroposophical Society are wasting opportunities all the time if we leave the printed Courses quite untouched and only want always to hear 'the latest' from the Goetheanum. And it will readily be understood that all possibility of printing the Courses would gradually cease if they were not widely made use of.

Another point of view also comes into consideration. In spreading the contents of Anthroposophy, a strong sense of responsibility is necessary in the first place. What is said about the spiritual world must be brought into a form such that the pictures of spiritual facts and beings which are given are not exposed to misunderstanding. Anyone who hears a lecture at the Goetheanum will receive an immediate and direct impression. If he repeats the contents of what he heard, this impression can echo from him; and he is able so to formulate them that they can be rightly understood. But if they are repeated at second or third hand, the possibility of inaccuracies creeping in becomes greater and greater. All these things should be borne in mind.

The following point of view is, however, probably the most important. The point is not that Anthroposophy should be simply listened to or read, but that it should be received into the living soul. It is essential that what has been received should be worked upon in thought and carried into the feelings; and the Leading Thoughts are really intended to suggest this with regard to the Courses already printed and in circulation. If this point of view is not sufficiently considered, then the nature of Anthroposophy will be constantly hindered from manifesting itself through the Anthroposophical Society. People say, though only with apparent justice: 'What use is it to me to hear all these things about the spiritual worlds if I cannot look into those worlds for myself?' One who speaks thus does not realise that such vision is promoted when the working out of anthroposophical ideas is thought of in the manner indicated above. The lectures at the Goetheanum are so given that their contents can live on and work freely in the minds of the hearers. The same applies also to the contents of the Courses. These do not contain dead material to be imparted externally, but material which, when viewed from different aspects, stimulates the vision for spiritual worlds. It should not be thought that one hears the contents of the lectures and that the knowledge of the spiritual world is acquired separately by means of meditation. In that way one will never make real progress. Both must act together in the soul. And to think out anthroposophical ideas and allow them to live on in the feelings is also an exercise of the soul. A person grows into the spiritual world with open eyes if he uses Anthroposophy in the manner we have described.

Far too little attention is paid in the Anthroposophical Society to the fact that Anthroposophy should not be abstract theory but real life. Real life, that is its nature; and if it is made into abstract theory this is often not at all a better but a worse theory than others. But it becomes theory only when it is made such—i.e., when one kills it. It is still not sufficiently realised that Anthroposophy is not only a conception of the world, different from others, but that *it must also be received differently*. Its nature is recognised and experienced only when one receives it in this different way.

The Goetheanum should be looked upon as the *necessary* centre of anthroposophical work and activity, but one ought not to lose sight of the fact that the anthroposophical material which has been worked out should also be made use of in the Groups. What is worked out at the Goetheanum can be obtained gradually by the whole Anthroposophical Society in a full and living sense, when as many members as possible come from the Groups to the Goetheanum itself and participate as much as possible in its activities.

But all this must be worked out with heart and mind; the mere imparting of the contents of the lectures each week is useless. The Executive at the Goetheanum will need time and will have to meet with sympathetic understanding on the part of the members. It will then be able to work in accordance with the intention of the Christmas Meeting.

Further Leading Thoughts issued from the Goetheanum for the Anthroposophical Society

76. To call forth an idea of the First Hierarchy (Seraphim, Cherubim and Thrones) we must try to create pictures in which the Spiritual—i.e. that which can be beheld only in the Supersensible—reveals its working, in forms that come to manifestation in the world of sense. Spiritual being, portrayed in sense-perceptible imagery: such must be the content of our thoughts about the First Hierarchy.

77. To call forth an idea of the Second Hierarchy (Kyriotetes, Dynamis, Exusiai) we must try to create pictures in which the Spiritual reveals itself—not in sense-perceptible forms—but in a purely spiritual way. Spiritual being, portrayed not in sense-perceptible but in purely spiritual imagery: such must be the content of our thoughts about the Second Hierarchy.

78. To call forth an idea of the Third Hierarchy (Archai, Archangeloi, Angeloi) we must try to create pictures in which the Spiritual reveals itself not in sense-perceptible forms, nor yet in a purely spiritual way, but in the way in which Thinking, Feeling and Willing come to expression in the human soul. Spiritual being, portrayed in the imagery of a life of soul: such must be the content of our thoughts about the Third Hierarchy.

Before and until the ninth century after the Mystery of Golgotha, the human being stood in a different relation to his thoughts from that which he has had in later times. He did not have the feeling that he himself brought forth the thoughts that lived in his soul. He regarded them as inspirations from a spiritual world. And when he had thoughts about what he perceived with his senses, even these thoughts were to him revelations of the Divine that spoke to him from the things of the senses.

Whoever has spiritual vision will understand this experience. For when something that is real in the spiritual sense communicates itself to the soul, one never has the feeling: 'There is the spiritual perception, and I myself am developing the thought with which to understand it.' But one *sees* the thought which the perception contains, and which is given with it, no less objectively than the perception itself.

(When dates are given in this connection, they are to be taken only as a rough indication of the period; the transition takes place quite gradually.) Speaking, in this sense, we may say that the ninth century saw the lighting-up, in the souls of men, of the individual personal intelligence.

Man began to have the feeling: '*I myself form my thoughts.*' And this forming of thoughts came to be the thing of first importance in the soul's life, so that man saw in the intellectual experience the very essence and being of his soul. In earlier times men had had an imaginative conception of the soul. To them the essential thing about the soul was not that it formed thoughts, but that it partook of the spiritual content of the Universe. It was the supersensible, spiritual Beings whom they conceived to be thinking, and—extending their influence into the human being—thinking into him as well. That which lives in the human being of the supersensible, spiritual world—this they felt as the soul.

As soon as we penetrate with higher vision into the

spiritual world, we meet with real and concrete spiritual Beings, spiritual Powers. In old teachings the Power from whom the thoughts in things proceed was designated by the name *Michael*. This name we may still apply, for it is true that human beings, once upon a time, received the thoughts of Michael. Michael held sway over the Cosmic Intelligence. But from the ninth century onwards men no longer felt that Michael was inspiring the thoughts into them. The thoughts had fallen away from his dominion—fallen out of the spiritual world into the individualised souls of men.

Henceforth it was within mankind that the life of thought was evolved. To begin with, men were uncertain as to what it was they had in their thoughts. This uncertainty found very real expression in the scholastic teachings. The Schoolmen were divided into Nominalists and Realists. The Realists, led by St. Thomas Aquinas and those who stood near to him, still felt the old closeness and kinship between thought and thing. Hence they saw in the thoughts a reality living in the things. They regarded the thoughts of man as reality which flows over from the things into the human soul.

The Nominalists felt very strongly the fact that the soul forms its thoughts. They felt that the thoughts were merely something that existed subjectively in the soul and had nothing to do with the objects. They were of the opinion that thoughts are only names man forms for things. (They did not speak of 'thoughts' but of 'universals,' but that does not come into consideration for the principle of the theory, as thoughts always contain something universal as compared with the individual objects.)

We may say that the Realists wished to remain faithful to Michael; even though the thoughts had fallen from his sphere into that of man, they wished, as thinkers, to serve Michael as the Ruler of the intelligence of the Cosmos. The Nominalists deserted Michael, with respect to the unconscious part of their soul. They did not consider Michael as the owner of the thoughts, but man.

Nominalism spread abroad and increased in influence up to the last third of the nineteenth century. Then at this period those persons who were able to perceive the spiritual events in the Universe felt that Michael had followed the stream of intellectual life. He is seeking a new metamorphosis of his cosmic task. Formerly he allowed the thoughts to stream from the spiritual outer world into the souls of men; since the last third of the nineteenth century he wishes to live *in* the human souls in which the thoughts are formed. In earlier times the human beings related to Michael saw him develop his activity in the spiritual sphere; they now know that they ought to let Michael dwell in their hearts; they now dedicate to him their spiritual life which is based upon thought; they now, in their free and individual life of thought, allow themselves to be instructed by Michael as to which are the right paths of the soul.

When those who in their former Earth-life received their thoughts by inspiration, i.e., who were servants of Michael, had returned to earthly life at the close of the nineteenth century, they felt urged towards a voluntary Michael community of this description. They now looked upon the one who had formerly inspired them with thoughts as their guide in forming higher thoughts.

One who understands how to observe such things knows what a great change took place in the last third of the nineteenth century with respect to the life of human thought. Before that time man could only feel how thoughts formed themselves in his own being; from the time indicated he is able to raise himself above his own being; he can turn his mind to the Spiritual; he there meets Michael, who proves his ancient kinship with everything connected with thought. He liberates thought from the sphere of the head; he clears the way for it to the heart; he enkindles enthusiasm in the feelings, so that the human mind can be filled with devotion for all that can be experienced in the *light of thought.*

The Age of Michael has dawned. Hearts are beginning to

have thoughts; spiritual fervour is now proceeding, not merely from mystical obscurity, but from souls clarified by thought. To understand this means to receive Michael into the heart. Thoughts which at the present time strive to grasp the Spiritual must originate in hearts which beat for Michael as the fiery Prince of Thought in the Universe.

Further Leading Thoughts issued from the Goetheanum for the Anthroposophical Society

79. Spiritually, we can approach the Third Hierarchy (Archai, Archangeloi, Angeloi) by learning to know Thinking, Feeling and Willing, so as to perceive in them the Spiritual that works in the soul. Thinking, to begin with, places not an effective reality, but only *pictures* into the world. Feeling lives and moves in this realm of pictures; bears witness to the presence of a reality in man, but cannot live it or express it outwardly. Willing unfolds a reality which presupposes the existence of the body but does not consciously assist in its formation. The spiritual reality that lives in our Thinking, to make the body the foundation of this Thinking; the spiritual reality that lives in our Feeling, to make the body share in the experience of a reality; the spiritual reality that lives in our Willing, consciously to assist in fashioning the body—all this is alive in the Third Hierarchy.

80. Spiritually, we can approach the Second Hierarchy (Exusiai, Dynamis, Kyriotetes) by awakening to see the facts of Nature as the manifestations of spiritual being that indwells them. The Second Hierarchy then has Nature for its dwelling-place, there to work upon the souls.

81. Spiritually, we can approach the First Hierarchy (Seraphim, Cherubim, Thrones) by awakening to see the facts that confront us in the kingdom of Nature and of Man

as the deeds (creations) of spiritual being that is working in them. The First Hierarchy then has the kingdom of Nature and of Man as the outcome of its work, wherein it unfolds its Being.

Further Leading Thoughts issued from the Goetheanum for the Anthroposophical Society

82. Man looks upward to the worlds of stars; what is there presented to his senses is but the outer manifestation of those Spirit-beings—and their deeds—of whom we have spoken as the Beings of the spiritual kingdoms or Hierarchies.

83. The Earth is the scene of action of the three Nature-kingdoms and of the human kingdom, inasmuch as these make manifest the outward and sensible glory of the activity of spiritual Beings.

84. The forces, working from spiritual Beings into the earthly kingdoms of Nature and into the kingdom of Man, are revealed to the human Spirit in the true—that is, the spiritual—knowledge of the starry worlds.

THE CONDITION OF THE HUMAN SOUL BEFORE THE DAWN OF THE MICHAEL AGE

To-day I will take the opportunity of giving some further thoughts in line with my article 'At the Dawn of the Michael Age'.

The Michael Age has taken its rise in the evolution of mankind at a time that follows on the one hand the predominance of the intellectual 'forming of thoughts,' and on the other hand the turning of human perception and vision to the outer world of the senses, to the physical world.

Thought-forming is in its nature *not* essentially an evolution in the direction of materialism. That which in bygone times came to the human being as something inspired into him, namely, the world of ideas, became, in the time that preceded the Michael epoch, the property of the human soul. The soul no longer receives the ideas 'from above' out of the spiritual content of the Cosmos: it draws them itself actively forth out of the human being's own spiritual nature. Man has thereby become ripe for reflection upon his own spiritual being. Hitherto he did not penetrate to these depths of his own nature. He saw in himself as it were a drop out of the sea of cosmic spirituality, a drop that has separated itself off for the time of this earthly life, only to unite itself again when the earthly life is over.

The thought-forming that goes on in the human being marks an advance in human self-knowledge. Viewed from the supersensible, it appears thus. The spiritual Powers that we may designate with the Michael-name held rule over the ideas in the spiritual Cosmos. The human being experienced these ideas by partaking with his soul in the life of the Michael-world. This experience has now become his own, and a temporary separation of the human being from the Michael-world has therewith come about. With the inspired thoughts of earlier times man received at the same time the content of the spiritual world. Since this inspiration has ceased and man now forms his thoughts from his own activity, he is referred to the perception of the senses to find a content for these thoughts. Thus was man obliged to fill with material content the spirituality that he had won. He fell into the materialistic outlook in the very epoch of time that brought his own spiritual being a stage higher in development.

This is easily liable to misunderstanding. We may observe only the 'fall' into materialism and lament over it. Whilst, however, the perception and vision of this age had to be limited to the external physical world, there was unfolding within the soul, as actual experience, a *purified and self-subsisting spirituality* of the human being. And now in the Michael Age this spirituality must no longer remain as unconscious *experience*, it must become conscious of its own proper nature. This signifies the entry of the Michael Being into the human soul. For a certain length of time man has filled his own spirit with the material side of Nature; he is to fill it again with cosmic content consisting of a spirituality that is his very own.

Thought-forming was lost for a time in the Matter of the Cosmos; it must be found again in the cosmic Spirit. Into the cold, abstract world of thought can enter warmth, can enter a spirit-reality that is filled with being. That represents the dawn of the Michael Age.

The consciousness of freedom could develop only in the depths of the human soul through this separation from the thought-being of the world. What came from the heights had to be found again in the depths. For this reason the development of the consciousness of freedom was connected first of all with a knowledge of Nature that was directed only to the external. While man was unconsciously developing his mind in the formation of clear ideas, his senses were directed outward solely to what is material, but this did not in any way disturb the tender seed that was beginning to germinate in the soul.

But the experience of the Spiritual, and together with it the *vision* of the Spiritual, can re-enter the vision of the outward material world in a new way. The knowledge of Nature acquired during the age of materialism can be comprehended in the soul's inner life in a spiritual way. Michael, who has spoken 'from above,' can be heard 'from within,' where he will begin to dwell. Speaking more imaginatively this may be expressed as follows: The Sun-nature which for long periods man received only from the Cosmos, will begin to shine within his soul. He will learn to speak of an 'inner Sun.' This will not prevent him from knowing himself to be an earthly being during his life between birth and death; but he will recognise that this his earthly being is *led by the Sun.* He will learn to feel as a truth, that a being places him, in his inner nature, into a light which shines indeed upon earthly existence but which is not enkindled within it. In the dawn of the Michael Age it may still seem as if all this were very far remote from humanity; but 'in the spirit' it is near; it only needs to be 'seen.' A very great deal depends upon this fact, that the ideas of man do not merely remain 'thinking,' but in thought develop *sight.*

Further Leading Thoughts issued from the Goethaenum for the Anthroposophical Society

85. It is in the waking day-consciousness that man experiences himself to begin with, during the present cosmic age. This experience conceals from him the fact that in this waking state the Third Hierarchy is present in his experience.

86. In the dream-consciousness man experiences, in a chaotic way, his own being unharmoniously united with the Spirit-being of the world. When the Imaginative Consciousness is realised as the other pole of the dream-consciousness,

man becomes aware that the Second Hierarchy is present in his experience.

87. In dreamless sleep-consciousness man experiences, all unconsciously, his own being united with the Spirit-being of the World. When the Inspired Consciousness is realised as the other pole of the sleep-consciousness, man becomes aware that the First Hierarchy is present in his experience.

APHORISMS FROM A LECTURE TO MEMBERS GIVEN IN LONDON ON AUGUST 24TH, 1924.

In the present stage of its evolution the human consciousness unfolds three forms, the waking, the dreaming, and the dreamless sleeping consciousness.

The waking consciousness experiences the outer world through the senses, forms ideas about it, and out of those ideas can create such as portray a purely spiritual world. The dreaming consciousness develops pictures in which the outer world is transformed, as, for instance, when the sun shining on the bed is experienced in dream as a conflagration in all its details. Or a man's own inner world may appear before him in symbolic pictures, as, for instance, the throbbing heart in the picture of an over-heated oven. Memories also re-appear transformed in the dream consciousness. What these memory pictures contain is not borrowed from the world of the senses, but from the spiritual world. However, it is not possible through the memory pictures to penetrate with understanding into the spiritual world, because they are just too dim to rise into the waking consciousness, and because what little may be perceived cannot be really understood.

But it is possible in the moment of waking to grasp so much of the dream world as to become aware that it is the imperfect copy of a spiritual experience which has happened in sleep, but which for the most part evades the waking consciousness. In order to comprehend this, it is only necessary to shape the moment of waking in such a way that the outer world is not conjured all at once before the soul, but that the soul, without as yet regarding the outer world, feels itself surrendered to what has been experienced within.

In the dreamless sleep consciousness the soul passes through experiences which mean nothing more for the memory than an indifferent period of time between falling asleep and waking.

These experiences may be spoken of as non-existent, until the way into them has been opened up through spiritual-scientific investigation. But if this takes place, if the Imaginative and Inspired consciousness described in anthroposophical literature be developed, then out of the darkness of sleep the pictures and inspirations belonging to the experience of previous lives on Earth make their appearance. It then becomes possible to survey also the content of the dream consciousness. This cannot be grasped by the waking consciousness; it has to do with the world in which man dwells as a disembodied soul between two earthly lives.

If one learns to know what is hidden behind the dream- and sleep-consciousness in the present age, then the way is clear to the understanding of the forms of human consciousness in past ages. One cannot, however, arrive at this by means of outer investigation; for evidence received from the outer world shows only the after-effects of the experiences of human consciousness in prehistoric times. Anthroposophical literature gives information as to how, by means of spiritual investigation, one may attain to the vision of such experiences.

It is found by means of spiritual research that in ancient Egyptian times man possessed a dream-consciousness which was much more like the waking consciousness than it is at the present day. The memory of the dream experiences passed into the waking consciousness, and the latter provided not only the sense impressions that can be grasped in clearly outlined thoughts, but in addition to these the Spiritual that is at work in the world of the senses. Man's consciousness thereby lived instinctively in the world he had left when he incarnated on the Earth—the world he will re-enter when he passes through the gate of death.

Inscribed monuments and other records preserved from ancient times give to those who penetrate them with an impartial mind, clear evidence of a consciousness of this kind, belonging to an age of which no outer relics exist.

In ancient Egyptian times the sleep-consciousness

contained dreams of the spiritual world, just as the sleep-consciousness of the present day contains dreams originating from the physical world. But among other peoples we find in addition another kind of consciousness. The experiences undergone during sleep passed over into the waking consciousness in such a way that there was an instinctive vision of repeated earthly lives. The traditions regarding the knowledge of repeated earthly lives possessed by ancient humanity originate from these forms of consciousness.

In the developed Imaginative consciousness we find again the dream-consciousness which in ancient times was dim and instinctive, only in the Imaginative consciousness it is fully conscious, like our waking life. And through the Inspired knowledge we become aware of the pre-historic instinctive insight which still saw something of the repeated earthly lives.

Modern writers of works on the history of humanity make no note of this transformation in the forms of human consciousness. They would like to believe that on the whole the present forms of consciousness have existed as long as humanity has been on the Earth. And what, in spite of this, does point to other forms of consciousness, viz., the myths and fairy-tales, they would prefer to look upon as the result of the poetic fantasy of primitive man.

Further Leading Thoughts issued from the Goetheanum for the Anthroposophical Society

88. In the waking day-consciousness man experiences himself, during the present cosmic age, standing in the midst of the physical world. This experience conceals from him the presence, within his being, of the effects of a life between death and birth.

89. In dream-consciousness man experiences, in a chaotic

way, his own being unharmoniously united with the spiritual being of the world. The waking consciousness cannot seize the real content of the dream-consciousness. To the Imaginative and Inspired Consciousness it is revealed how the Spirit-world through which man lives between death and birth is helping to build up his inner being.

90. In dreamless sleep-consciousness man experiences, all unconsciously, his own being permeated with the results of past earthly lives. The Inspired and Intuitive Consciousness penetrates to a clear vision of these results, and sees the working of former earthly lives in the destined course—the Karma—of the present.

Further Leading Thoughts issued from the Goetheanum for the Anthroposophical Society

91. The Will enters the ordinary consciousness, in the present cosmic age, only through Thought. Now in this consciousness we always have to take our start from something sense-perceptible. Thus, even of our own Will, we apprehend only what passes from it into the world of sense-perceptions. In the ordinary consciousness it is only by observation of himself in thought that man is aware of his Will-impulses, just as it is only by observation that he is aware of the outer world.

92. The Karma that works in the Will is a property belonging to it from former lives on Earth. This constituent of the Will cannot therefore be apprehended with the ideas of our ordinary sense-existence, which are directed only to the present earthly life.

93. Because they are unable to take hold of Karma, these ideas refer what is unintelligible to them in man's impulses

of Will to the mystic darkness of the bodily constitution, whereas in reality it is the working of past earthly lives.

Further Leading Thoughts issued from the Goentheanum for the Anthroposophical Society

94. With the ordinary life in ideas transmitted through the senses, man is in the physical world. For this world to enter his consciousness, Karma must be silent in his thinking life. In his life of ideation, man as it were *forgets his Karma.*

95. In the manifestations of the Will, Karma works itself out. But its working remains in the unconscious. By lifting to conscious Imagination what works unconsciously in the Will, Karma is apprehended. Man feels his destiny within him.

96. When Inspiration and Intuition enter the Imagination, then, beside the impulses of the present, the outcome of former earthly lives becomes perceptible in the working of the Will. The past life is revealed, working itself out in the present.

Further Leading Thoughts issued from the Goetheanum for the Anthroposophical Society

97. For a cruder description it is permissible to say: Thinking, Feeling and Willing live in the soul of man. For greater refinement we must add: Thinking always contains a substratum of Feeling and Willing; Feeling a substratum of Thinking and Willing; Willing a substratum of Thinking and Feeling. In the life of thought, however, Thinking predominates; in the life of feeling, Feeling predominates; and in the life of will, Willing predominates over the other contents of the soul.

98. The Feeling and Willing of the life of Thought contain the karmic outcome of past lives on Earth. The Thinking and Willing of the life of Feeling karmically determine the man's character. The Thinking and Feeling of the life of Will tear the present earthly life away from Karmic connections.

99. In the Feeling and Willing of Thinking man lives out his Karma of the past; in the Thinking and Feeling of Willing he prepares his Karma of the future.

Further Leading Thoughts issued from the Goetheanum for the Anthroposophical Society

100. The thoughts of man have their true seat in the etheric body. There, however, they are forces of real life and being. They imprint themselves upon the physical body, and as such 'imprinted thoughts' they have the shadowy character in which the everyday consciousness knows them.

101. The Feeling that lives in the Thoughts comes from the astral body, and the Willing from the Ego. In sleep the human etheric body is certainly irradiated with the world of his Thoughts, but man himself does not partake in it. For he has withdrawn, with the astral body the Feeling of the Thoughts, and with the Ego their Willing, out of the etheric and the physical.

102. The moment the astral body and Ego loose their connection during sleep with the Thoughts of the etheric body, they enter into connection with 'Karma'—with the beholding of the events through repeated lives on Earth. To the everyday consciousness this vision is denied, but a supersensible consciousness can enter into it.

It is not possible to perceive in the right light how the Michael Impulse breaks into human evolution, if one shares the conception which is universally accepted to-day, as to the relation of the new world of ideas to Nature.

It is thought: There outside us is Nature with all that she accomplishes and is; within us are the ideas. These ideas are thoughts about the things of Nature, or about the so-called Laws of Nature. The thinkers of to-day are concerned first of all to show how to form such ideas as shall stand in a true relation to Nature, or in which the true Natural Laws shall be contained.

It is of little importance to them how these ideas are related to the man himself, who has them. But in truth there can be no real insight until this question is raised: What does Man experience through the natural-scientific ideas of modern times?

The answer can be arrived at in the following way.

Man feels to-day that the ideas are formed within him through the activity of his soul. He has the feeling that he himself forms his ideas, while only the sense-perceptions come to him from without.

Man did not always feel in this way. In times past he did not realise the content of his ideas as something he had made himself, but as something received through inspiration from the supersensible world.

There were various stages of this feeling. And these stages depended on that part of a man's being in which he experienced what to-day he calls his ideas. To-day, in the period of the development of the Spiritual Soul or Consciousness-Soul, what is contained in the 'Leading Thoughts' of the last number is wholly true:—Thoughts have their true seat in the human etheric body. There, however, they are real, living forces. They imprint themselves in the physical body, and as such "imprinted thoughts" they possess the shadowy character known to ordinary consciousness.

Now one can go back to times in which the thoughts were directly experienced in the 'Ego.' But in those times they were not shadowy as they are to-day, nor were they merely living; they were full of soul and spirit. But this means that the man did not only *think* his thoughts; he had as an experience the perception of concrete spiritual beings.

Everywhere amongst the peoples of antiquity one finds the consciousness that looked up to a world of spiritual beings. The historical remains of this are described to-day as a consciousness that expressed itself in myths and mythologies, which are not considered of much importance for an understanding of the real world. And yet with this consciousness man stands in his own world—in the world of his true origin—whereas with his present consciousness he is lifted out of his own world. Man is a spirit; and *his* world is the world of spiritual beings.

The next stage was one in which the element of thought was no longer experienced by the Ego but by the astral body. The soul here loses the direct vision of the Spiritual. Thought appears as an element which is ensouled and alive.

At the first stage, that of the vision of concrete spiritual beings, man does not feel at all strongly the necessity of connecting what he sees with that which he perceives through his senses. The phenomena perceptible to the senses are seen to be the deeds of what he observes supersensibly, but he does not feel impelled to develop a special science of that which is directly seen by spiritual vision. Moreover, the world of spirit-beings which he sees is so rich that his attention is directed to it above all things.

It is different at the second stage of consciousness. Here the concrete spiritual beings are hidden; their reflection appears in the form of an ensouled life. Man begins to relate the 'life of Nature' to this 'life of souls.' In the beings and processes of Nature he seeks the active spirit-beings and their deeds. The result of this stage of consciousness may be seen historically in that which appeared later as the quest of the alchemists.

When at the first stage of consciousness man 'thought' the spirit-beings, he lived entirely in his own being; and at the second stage, too, he is still quite near to his origin. But at both stages it is quite impossible for man to develop, in the true sense of the word, his own inner impulses of action.

A spirituality which is of like nature with himself acts in him. What *he* seems to do is the manifestation of processes which come about through spirit-beings. What man does is the sensibly physical manifestation of a real spiritual and divine event which stands behind.

A third epoch in the development of consciousness brings thought to consciousness in the etheric body, but as living thought.

The Greeks lived in this consciousness when Greek civilisation was at its prime. The ancient Greek did not form thoughts for himself and then look out upon the world with them as with his own creations, but when he thought he felt that a life was being kindled within him—a life which also pulsated in the objects and events outside him.

Then for the first time there arose in man the longing for the freedom of his own actions—not yet true freedom, but the longing for it.

Man, who felt the life and activity of Nature asserting itself in him, could develop the longing to detach his own activity from the activity which he perceived outside him and around him. But after all, this outer activity was still perceived as the final result of the active spirit-world, which is of like nature with man himself.

Only when the thoughts were imprinted in the physical body and when the consciousness extended only to this imprint—then only did the possibility of freedom arise. This condition came with the fifteenth century A.D.

For the evolution of the world the important point is not, 'What is the significance of the ideas of modern natural science with regard to Nature?' For in effect these ideas have assumed their forms, not in order to provide man with a certain picture of Nature, but in order to bring him forward to a certain stage in his evolution.

When thoughts laid hold of the physical body, spirit, soul and life had been excluded from their immediate contents, and the abstract shadow attaching to the physical body alone remained. Thoughts such as these can make *only* what is physical and material into the object of their knowledge, for they themselves are only *real* in the physical and material body of man. Materialism did not originate because material beings and processes alone can be perceived in external Nature, but because man had to pass through a stage in his development which led him to a consciousness at first only capable of seeing material manifestations. The one-sided development of this necessity in human evolution resulted in the modern view of Nature.

It is Michael's mission to bring into human etheric bodies the forces through which the thought-shadows may regain *life*; then the souls and spirits in the supersensible worlds will incline towards the enlivened thoughts, and the liberated human being will be able to live with them, just as formerly the human being who was only the physical image of *their* activity lived with them.

Further Leading Thoughts issued from the Goetheanum for the Anthroposophical Society

103. In the evolution of mankind consciousness descends on the ladder of unfolding Thought. There was an earliest stage in consciousness when man experienced the Thoughts in the Ego—experienced them as real Beings, imbued with Spirit, soul and life. At a second stage he experienced the Thoughts in the astral body; henceforth they appeared only as the images of Spirit-beings—images, however, still imbued with

soul and life. At a third stage he experienced the Thoughts in the etheric body; here they manifest only an inner stirring, like an echo of the quality of soul. At the fourth, which is the present stage, man experiences the Thoughts in the physical body, where they appear as the dead shadows of the Spiritual.

104. In like measure as the quality of Spirit, soul and life in human Thought recedes, man's own Will comes to life. True freedom becomes possible.

105. It is the task of Michael to lead man back again, on paths of Will, whence he came down when with his earthly consciousness he descended on the paths of Thought from the living experience of the Supersensible to the experience of the world of sense.

When man looks back on his evolution, and calls up before his inner eye the special characteristics which his spiritual life has assumed for the last five hundred years, he cannot help recognising, even within the ordinary consciousness and if but faintly, that since this period the whole earthly evolution of man stands at a significant and critical point.

In the last study I referred from one point of view to this significant turning-point. One looks up from this point into the distant past of evolution; one sees how the soul-force in man which to-day is active as the force of intelligence, has changed in the course of time.

In the present period, thoughts—dead abstract thoughts—make their appearance in the field of human consciousness. These thoughts are bound up with the physical body of man; man is obliged to recognise that they are of his own generating.

In primitive times, when man turned his soul in the direction in which to-day his thoughts are revealed to him, he saw Divine-Spiritual Beings. He knew himself bound to these Beings in his whole nature, even down to the physical body; he was obliged to recognise himself as their offspring. But he not only owed his *being* to them, he also owed them what he *accomplished.* Man had no will of his own. What he did was a manifestation of Divine Will.

By degrees, as described in the last study, man attained to a will of his own, at a period which dawned about five hundred years ago.

But this stage was far more different from all those which preceded it than any of them from one another.

When the thoughts pass over into the physical body, they lose their livingness. They are dead forms, spiritually dead. Previously, though belonging to man, they were at the same time organs of the Divine-Spiritual Beings to whom man belonged. They were actual *will* in man. And through them the man felt himself in living union with the spiritual world.

With his dead thoughts he felt himself cut off from the spiritual world. He felt himself entirely removed to the physical world.

But this means also that he is now in the sphere of the Ahrimanic spirituality. The Ahrimanic spirituality had no great power in the regions in which the Beings of the higher Hierarchies retained man as in their own sphere—when as in primitive ages the higher Beings themselves acted directly in man, or when, as in later times, they worked in him through their ensouled or living reflection. As long as this working of supersensible Beings within the doings of man continued—that is until about the fifteenth century—the Ahrimanic powers had, *within the evolution of mankind*, only a faintly echoing power, if one may express it so.

The description of Ahriman's activity given in the Persian religion is not in contradiction with this statement. For that religion refers to Ahriman's activity, not within the human soul, but in a world bordering directly upon the world of the human soul. Ahriman's action, as there described, does indeed affect the world of the human soul from a neighbouring spirit-world, but it does not directly interfere.

This direct interference has only become possible in the space of time which began about five hundred years ago.

Thus man is at the close of a stream of evolution within which his nature has developed out of a divine spirituality which finally dies *to itself* in the abstract intelligence of man.

Man has not remained in the divine-spiritual spheres in which he originated.

What began five hundred years ago for the consciousness of man had already taken place for a wider sphere of his whole being at the time when the Mystery of Golgotha took place on the Earth. It was then that, imperceptibly to the consciousness of the majority of human beings at that time, human evolution gradually glided out of a world in which Ahriman has little power, into one in which his power is great. This gliding into a different stratum of the world was completed in the fifteenth century.

Ahriman's influence upon man in this stratum of the world is possible and can act so destructively because the activity of the Gods related to man has died in this sphere. But man could not develop free-will in any other way than by entering a sphere in which the Divine-Spiritual Beings connected with him from the very beginning were not alive.

Considered cosmically, the Mystery of the Sun is contained in the nature of this evolution of humanity. The Divine-Spiritual Beings connected with his origin were united with that which—up to that important turning-point in his evolution—man was able to perceive in the Sun. These Divine-Spiritual Beings have separated from the Sun and have left there only the part of them that has died, so that the bodily nature of man can now receive through the Sun only the power of dead thoughts.

But these Beings have sent Christ from the Sun to the Earth. For the welfare of humanity Christ has united His being with the dead part of divine-spiritual existence in Ahriman's kingdom. Thus two things are possible for man, and through this possibility his freedom is guaranteed:—to turn to Christ consciously in the spiritual frame of mind which he possessed subconsciously during the descent from the vision of supersensible spirit-existence to the use of intellect; or to wish to feel his severance from spirit-existence and thus fall in the direction taken by the Ahrimanic powers.

Humanity has been in this situation since the beginning of the fifteenth century. It was prepared—for everything takes place gradually in evolution—after the Mystery of Golgotha, which, as it is the greatest event that has happened on the Earth, is destined to rescue man from the destruction to which he must be exposed because he is to become a free being.

Now we may say that what has hitherto been done by

humanity itself within this situation has taken place half-unconsciously. It has led to what is good in the modern Nature-conception which lives in abstract thought, and it has led to many practical principles of life, equally good.

But the age in which man could unfold his life thus unconsciously in the dangerous sphere of Ahriman has come to an end.

It is the duty of the investigator into the spiritual world to draw the attention of humanity to the spiritual fact that Michael has taken over the spiritual guidance of human affairs. Michael does what he has to do in such a way that he does not thereby wield an influence over human beings; but they may follow him in freedom, in order with the Christ-power to find the way out of that sphere of Ahriman which they were obliged to enter.

One who honestly, out of the deepest being of his soul, can feel himself one with Anthroposophy, understands this phenomenon of Michael truly. And Anthroposophy would like to be the message of this mission of Michael.

Further Leading Thoughts issued from the Goetheanum for the Anthroposophical Society

106. Michael goes upward again along the paths by which mankind descended, stage by stage in the evolution of the Spirit, down to the exercise of the Intelligence. Michael, however, will lead the Will upward, retracing the paths by which the Wisdom descended to the final stage of Intelligence.

107. From this moment onward in world-evolution, Michael merely *shows* his way, so that man may follow it in perfect freedom. This distinguishes the present guidance by Michael from all preceding guidances of the Archangels, including even those of Michael himself. For the former guidances did

not only reveal their working. They worked themselves out in man. Hence in the working of his own life man could not be free.

108. To see and understand that this is so: this is the present task of man. For then he will find, with all the forces of his soul, his spiritual path within the Age of Michael.

THE EXPERIENCES OF MICHAEL IN THE COURSE OF HIS COSMIC MISSION

It is possible to follow the progress of mankind from the point of view of man himself, from the stage of consciousness in which he felt himself as a member of the Divine-Spiritual order, up to the present time, when he is conscious of himself as an individual, freed from the Divine-Spiritual, and able to think for himself. In our last study this point of view was taken.

But it is also possible, through supersensible vision, to make a picture of what Michael and those who belong to him experience during this evolutionary process—i.e., to describe the facts of it as they appear to Michael himself. This shall now be attempted.

There is an earliest epoch in evolution, where it is only possible to speak of what takes place among Divine-Spiritual Beings. Here one has to deal with the actions of the Gods alone. Gods fulfil what the impulses of their natures inspire, and are satisfied in this their activity. What they themselves experience in all this is alone important. But in one corner of this field of the Gods' activity, something resembling mankind is to be observed, as forming a part of their divine activity.

The spiritual Being who from the beginning directed his gaze towards mankind is Michael. He so orders the divine activities that in one part of the Cosmos mankind may exist. And his own activity is of the same nature as that which is revealed later in man as intellect; but this intellect is active as a force that streams through the Cosmos, ordering ideas and giving rise to actual realities. In this force Michael works. His office is to rule the cosmic intellectuality. And he wills the further progress in his domain, which consists in this:—that that which works as intelligence throughout the whole Cosmos should later become concentrated within the human individuality. As a result the following takes place:—there comes a time in the evolution of the world when the Cosmos subsists no longer on its own present intelligence, but on the cosmic intelligence belonging to the past. For the present intelligence must then be sought in the stream of human evolution.

What Michael desires is to keep the intelligence, which is developing within humanity, permanently in connection with the Divine-Spiritual Beings.

But in this he is meeting with opposition. What the Gods accomplish in their evolution, in that they release the cosmic intellectuality so that it may become a part of human nature, stands revealed as a fact within the world. If there are beings with power to perceive this fact, then they can take advantage of it. And such beings do indeed exist. They are the Ahrimanic beings. It is their nature to absorb into themselves all that comes forth from the Gods as intelligence. They have the capacity to unite with their own being the sum-total of all intellectuality, and thus they become the greatest, the most comprehensive and penetrating intelligences in the Cosmos.

Michael foresees how man, in progressing more and more towards his own individual use of intelligence, must meet with these Ahrimanic beings, and how by uniting with them he may then succumb to them. For this reason Michael brings the Ahrimanic Powers under his feet; he continually thrusts them into a deeper region than the one in which man is evolving. Michael, thrusting the dragon at his feet into the abyss: that is the mighty picture which lives in human consciousness of the supersensible facts here described.

Evolution progresses. The intellectuality which was at first entirely in the sphere of divine spirituality, detaches itself so far that it becomes the element which ensouls the Cosmos. That which previously had only radiated from the Gods themselves now shines as the manifestation of the Divine from the world of the stars. Formerly the world had been guided by the Divine Being himself: it is now guided by the Divine manifestation which has become objective, and behind this manifestation the Divine Being passes through the next stage of his own development.

Michael is again the ruler of the cosmic intelligence, in so far as this streams through the manifestations of the Cosmos in the order of ideas.

The third phase of evolution is a further separation of the cosmic intelligence from its origin. In the worlds of the stars the present order of ideas no longer holds sway as the Divine manifestation; the stars move and are regulated according to the order of ideas implanted in them in the past. Michael sees how the cosmic intellectuality, which he has hitherto ruled in the Cosmos, proceeds on its way to earthly humanity.

But Michael also sees how the danger of humanity succumbing to the Ahrimanic Powers grows greater and greater. He knows that *as regards himself* he will always have Ahriman under his feet; but will it also be the case with man?

Michael sees the greatest event in the Earth's history taking place. From the kingdom served by Michael himself Christ descends to the sphere of the Earth, so as to be there when the intelligence is wholly with the human individuality. For man will then feel most strongly the impulse to devote himself to the power which has made itself fully and completely into the vehicle of intellectuality. But Christ will be there; through His great sacrifice He will live in the same sphere in which Ahriman also lives. Man will be able to choose between Christ and Ahriman. The world will be able to find the Christ-way in the evolution of humanity.

That is Michael's cosmic experience with that which he has to govern in the Cosmos. In order to remain with that which he has to govern, he enters upon the path that leads from the Cosmos to humanity. He has been on this path since the eighth century A.D., but he really only took up his earthly office, into which his cosmic office has been changed, in the last third of the nineteenth century.

Michael cannot force human beings to do anything. For it is just through intelligence having come entirely into the sphere of the human individuality that compulsion has ceased. But in the supersensible world first bordering on this visible world, Michael can unfold as a majestic, exemplary action that which he wishes to display. He can show himself there with an aura of light, with the gesture of a Spirit-Being, in which all the splendour and glory of the past intelligence of the Gods is revealed. He can there show how the action of this intelligence of the past is more true, more beautiful and more virtuous in the present than all that is contained in the immediate intelligence of the present day, which streams to us from Ahriman in deceptive, misleading splendour. He can point out how for him Ahriman will always be the lower spirit, under his feet.

Those persons who can see the supersensible world bordering next upon the visible world, perceive Michael and those belonging to him in the manner here described, engaged in what they would like to do for humanity. Such persons see how—through the picture of Michael in Ahriman's sphere—man is to be led in freedom away from Ahriman to Christ. When through their vision such persons also succeed in opening the hearts and minds of others, so that there is a circle of people who know how Michael is now living among men, humanity will then begin to celebrate Festivals of Michael which will possess the right contents, and at which souls will allow the power of Michael to revive in them. Michael will then work as a real power among men. Man will be free and yet proceed along his spiritual path of life through the Cosmos in intimate companionship with Christ.

Further Leading Thoughts issued from the Goetheanum for the Anthroposophical Society (with reference to the preceding study)

109. To become truly conscious of the working of Michael

in the spiritual order of the World, is to solve the riddle of human freedom in relation to the Cosmos, in so far as the solution is necessary for man on Earth.

110. For 'Freedom' as a fact is directly given to every human being who understands himself in the present period of mankind's evolution. No one can say, 'Freedom is not,' unless he wishes to deny a patent fact. But we can find a certain contradiction between this fact of our experience and the processes of the Cosmos. In contemplating the mission of Michael within the Cosmos this contradiction is dissolved.

111. In my *Philosophy of Freedom* (Philosophy of Spiritual Activity) the 'Freedom' of the human being in the present world-epoch is proved as an essential element of consciousness. In the descriptions here given of the Mission of Michael, the cosmic foundations of the 'coming-into-being' of this Freedom are disclosed.

THE ACTIVITY OF MICHAEL AND THE FUTURE OF MANKIND

How does man stand to-day in his present stage of evolution with respect to Michael and his hosts?

Man is surrounded to-day by a world which was once of a wholly divine-spiritual nature—divine-spiritual being of which he also was a member. Thus at that time the world belonging to man was a world of divine-spiritual being. But this was no longer so in a later stage of evolution. The world had then become a cosmic manifestation of the Divine-Spiritual; the Divine Being hovered behind the manifestation. Nevertheless, the Divine-Spiritual lived and moved in all that was thus manifested. A world of stars was already there, in the light and movement of which the Divine-Spiritual lived and moved and manifested itself. One may say that at that time, in the position or movement of a star, the activity of the Divine and Spiritual was directly evident.

And in all this—in the working of the Divine Spirit in the Cosmos, and in the life of man resulting from this divine activity—Michael was as yet in his own element—unhindered, unresisted. The adjustment of the relation between the Divine and the Human was in his hands.

But other ages dawned. The world of the stars ceased to be a direct and present manifestation of Divine-Spiritual activity. The constellations lived and moved, maintaining what the Divine activity had been in them in the past. The Divine-Spiritual dwelt in the Cosmos in manifestation no longer, but in the manner of its working only. There was now a certain distinct separation between the Divine-Spiritual and the cosmic World. Michael, by virtue of his own nature, adhered to the Divine-Spiritual, and endeavoured to keep mankind as closely as possible in touch with it.

This he continued to do, more and more. His will was to preserve man from living too intensely in a world which represents only the Working of the Divine and Spiritual—which is not the real Being, nor its Manifestation.

It is a deep source of satisfaction to Michael that through man himself he has succeeded in keeping the world of the stars in direct union with the Divine and Spiritual. For when man, having fulfilled his life between death and a new birth, enters on the way to a new Earth-life, in his descent he seeks to establish a harmony between the course of the stars and his coming life on Earth. In olden times this harmony existed as a matter of course, because the Divine-Spiritual was active in the stars, where human life too had its source. But to-day, when the course of the stars is only a continuing of the manner in which the Divine-Spiritual worked in the past, this harmony could not exist unless man sought it. Man brings his divine-spiritual portion—which he has preserved from the past—into relation with the stars, which now only bear their divine-spiritual nature within them as an after-working from an earlier time.

In this way there comes into man's relation to the world something of the Divine, which corresponds to former ages and yet appears in these later times. *That this is so, is the deed of Michael.* And this deed gives him such deep satisfaction that in it he finds a portion of his very life, a portion of his sunlike, living energy.

But at the present time, when Michael directs his spiritual eyes to the Earth, he sees another fact as well—very different from the above. During his physical life between birth and death man has a world around him in which even the *Working* of the Divine-Spiritual no longer appears directly, but only something which has remained over as its result;—we may describe it by saying it is only the accomplished Work of the Divine-Spiritual. This accomplished Work, in all its forms, is essentially of a Divine and Spiritual kind. To human vision the Divine is manifested in the forms and in the processes of Nature; but it is *no longer* indwelling as a living principle. Nature is this divinely accomplished work of God; Nature everywhere around us is an image of the Divine Working.

In this world of sunlike Divine glory, but no longer livingly Divine, man dwells. Yet as a result of Michael's working upon him man has maintained his connection with the essential Being of the Divine and Spiritual. He lives as a being permeated by God in a world that is no longer permeated by God.

Into this world that has become empty of God, man will carry what is in him—what his being has become in this present age.

Humanity will evolve into a new world-evolution. The Divine and Spiritual from which man originates can become the cosmically expanding Human Being, radiating with a new light through the Cosmos which now exists only as an image of the Divine and Spiritual.

The Divine Being which will thus shine forth through Humanity will no longer be the same Divine Being which was once the Cosmos. In its passage through Humanity the Divine-Spiritual will come to a realisation of Being which it could not manifest before.

The Ahrimanic Powers try to prevent evolution from taking the course here described. It is not their will that the original Divine-Spiritual Powers should illumine the Universe in its further course. They want the cosmic intellectuality which they themselves have absorbed to radiate through the whole of the new Cosmos, and in this intellectualised and Ahrimanised Cosmos they want man to live on.

Were he to live such a life man would lose Christ. For Christ came into the world with an Intellectuality that is still of the very same essence as once lived in the Divine-Spiritual, when the Divine-Spiritual in its own Being still informed the Cosmos. But if at the present time we speak in such a manner that our thoughts can also be the thoughts of

Christ, we set over against the Ahrimanic Powers something which can save us from succumbing to them.

To understand the meaning of Michael's mission in the Cosmos is to be able to speak in this way. In the present time we must be able to speak of Nature in the way demanded by the evolutionary stage of the Consciousness Soul or Spiritual Soul. We must be able to receive into ourselves the purely natural-scientific way of thinking. But we ought also to learn to feel and speak about Nature in a way that is according to Christ. We ought to learn the Christ-Language—not only about redemption from Nature, about the soul and things Divine—but about the things of the Cosmos.

When with inward, heartfelt feeling we realise the mission and the deeds of Michael and those belonging to him, when we enter into all that they are in our midst, then we shall be able to maintain our human connection with the Divine and Spiritual origin, and understand how to cultivate the Christ-Language about the Cosmos. For to understand Michael is to find the way in our time to the Logos, as lived by Christ here on Earth and among men.

Anthroposophy truly values what the natural-scientific way of thinking has learned to say about the world during the last four or five centuries. But in addition to this language it speaks another, about the nature of man, about his evolution and that of the Cosmos; for it would fain speak the language of Christ and Michael.

If both these languages are spoken it will not be possible for evolution to be broken off or to pass over to Ahriman before the original Divine-Spiritual is found. To speak only in the natural-scientific way corresponds to the separation of intellectuality from the original Divine and Spiritual. This *can* indeed lead over into the Ahrimanic realm if Michael's mission remains unobserved. But *it will not do so* if through the power of Michael's example the intellect which has become free finds itself again in the original cosmic intellectuality, which has separated from man and become objective to him. For that cosmic intellectuality lies in the original source of man, and it appeared in Christ in full reality of being within the sphere of humanity, after it had left man for a time so that he might unfold his freedom.

Further Leading Thoughts issued from the Goetheanum for the Anthroposophical Society (with reference to the preceding study)

112. The Divine-Spiritual comes to expression in the Cosmos in different ways, in succeeding stages: (1) through its own and inmost *Being*; (2) through the *Manifestation* of this Being; (3) through the *active Working*, when the Being withdraws from the Manifestation; (4) through the *accomplished Work*, when in the outwardly apparent Universe no longer the Divine itself, but only the forms of the Divine are there.

113. In the modern conception of Nature man has no relation to the Divine, but only to the accomplished Work. With all that is imparted to the human soul by this science of Nature, man can unite himself either with the powers of Christ or with the dominions of Ahriman.

114. Michael is filled with the striving—working through his example in perfect freedom—to embody in human cosmic evolution the relation to the Cosmos which is still preserved in man himself from the ages when the Divine Being and the Divine Manifestation held sway. In this way, all that is said by the modern view of Nature—relating as it does purely to the image, purely to the form of the Divine—will merge into a higher, spiritual view of Nature. The latter will indeed exist in man; but it will be an echo in human experience of the Divine relation to the Cosmos which prevailed in the first two stages of cosmic evolution. This is how Anthroposophy confirms the view of Nature which the age of the Spiritual Soul has evolved, while supplementing it with that which is revealed to spiritual seership.

When with deep and earnest feeling a human being takes the inner vision of Michael's being and his deeds into his outlook on life, there will dawn upon him the true understanding of the way in which this world is to be taken by man—this world which is neither the Divine Being, nor the Manifestation, nor Active Working, but the *Accomplished Work* of the Gods. To look with knowledge into this world is to have before us forms and formations which speak aloud of the Divine; in which, however—if we are under no illusion about it—independent, living, Divine Being cannot be found. Nor must we consider merely our knowledge of the world. It is true that with respect to knowledge this configuration of the world, as it surrounds man at the present day, is revealed most strikingly. But more essential for everyday life is our feeling, our willing and work in a world which—though in its formation we may well feel it to be Divine—cannot really be experienced as actively imbued with Divine life. In order to bring real moral life into such a world, the ethical impulses I have described in my book *The Philosophy of Freedom* are necessary.

For the man who feels truly, Michael's Being and his present world of deeds can shine forth in this world of the Divine accomplished work. Michael does not enter into the physical world as a phenomenal appearance. He keeps himself with all his activity within a supersensible region—albeit one which borders directly upon the physical world of the present phase of world-evolution. Thus it can never happen that men's view of Nature will be led away into the fantastic through the impressions they receive from the Being of Michael; nor will they be inclined thereby to shape their ethical and practical life in this world—Divine as it is in its form, but void of Divine life—as if impulses could be there in it which did not require to be sustained, ethically and spiritually, by man himself. If we transplant ourselves into the Spiritual, be it in thinking or in willing, we shall always be obliged to approach Michael.

We shall thereby live spiritually in the following way. We shall accept both our knowledge and our life in the manner in which we are obliged to accept them since the fifteenth century. But we shall hold fast to Michael's revelation. We shall let this revelation shine like a light into the thoughts we receive from Nature; we shall carry it as warmth in our hearts when we have to live in accordance with a world which is the accomplished work of the Divine. We shall then place before us not only the observation and experience of the present world but also that which Michael makes possible for us, namely a past condition of the world—one which Michael, through his Being and his deeds, brings into the present.

If it were otherwise—if Michael were to work in such a manner that he carried his deeds into the world which at the present time man must know and experience as the physical—man would now learn of the world, not that which in reality *is* in it but that which *was* in it. This illusory conception of the world, when it takes place, leads the human soul away from the reality that is suited to it and into another—into a Luciferic one.

The manner in which Michael brings the past into activity in present human life is the one which is in accordance with the true spiritual progress of the world and contains nothing Luciferic. It is important that in the human mind there should be a correct idea of the way in which, in Michael's mission, everything Luciferic is avoided.

To have this attitude towards the light of Michael which is dawning in human history means at the same time to be able to find the right way to Christ.

Michael will point out the right road with respect to the world which lies about man, for him to know and be active in it. The way to Christ will have to be found *within.*

It is quite comprehensible that, during the period in

which the knowledge of Nature has the form given to it by the last five centuries, the knowledge of the supersensible world should also have become such as humanity now experiences.

Nature has to be known and experienced in such a manner that the Gods are nowhere in it. In consequence of this, man in this form of his relation to the world, experiences himself no longer. Inasmuch as he is a supersensible being, the position of his Self with respect to Nature which is in accordance with this age yields him nothing at all regarding his own being. Nor, if he has this position alone in view, can he live ethically in a manner in keeping with his true humanity.

Naturally, this causes people to prevent the modern way of knowledge and of life from entering into anything that relates to the supersensible nature of man, nay to the supersensible world at all. They separate this latter realm from anything accessible to human knowledge. A sphere of Revelation by Faith, apart from science or above it, is set up in contradistinction to the sphere of what is knowable.

But over against this there stands the purely spiritual activity of Christ, who since the Mystery of Golgotha can be reached by the human soul. The soul's relation to Christ need not remain indefinite or dimly mystical in feeling; it can become one that is quite concrete, humanly deep and clearly experienced.

Then, from the life together with Christ, there flows into the human soul what it ought to know regarding its own supersensible being. The religious revelation must then be felt in such a manner that the living experience of Christ continually streams into it. It will become possible for life to be filled with Christ, through Christ being perceived as the Being who gives to the human soul the knowledge of its own supersensible nature.

Thus the Michael experience and the Christ experience will in the future be able to stand side by side. Through

Michael man will find the path into the supersensible world in the right way with respect to the outer world of Nature. Our view of Nature, without being falsified in itself, will then be able to stand by the side of a spiritual view of the world and of man inasmuch as he is a cosmic being.

Through his true attitude to Christ man will be able, in the active intercourse of his soul with Christ, to experience what he could otherwise only receive as a traditional revelation by faith. He will be able to experience the inner world of the soul's life as one that is shone through by the Spirit; and he will also experience the outer world of Nature as one that is upborne by the Spirit.

If man were to gain information about his own supersensible nature without his life in union with Christ, this would lead him out of his own reality and into that of Ahriman. Christ bears within Himself, in a manner true to the whole Cosmos, the impulses for the future of humanity. To unite with Christ signifies for the human soul to receive into itself, in a manner true to the Cosmos, its own seeds for the future. Other beings who already at the present time manifest forms which will be cosmically right for man only in the future, belong to the Ahrimanic sphere. To unite ourselves with Christ in the right way is also to preserve ourselves in the right way from the Ahrimanic.

Those who strictly demand that the revelations of religious faith shall be preserved from the invasions of human knowledge are unconsciously afraid that by such ways as this man might come under Ahrimanic influences. This fact must be appreciated. But it should also be appreciated that it is to the honour and true recognition of Christ when that gift of grace, which is the inflowing of the Spiritual into the human soul, is ascribed to the living experience with Him.

Thus in the future the Michael experience and the Christ experience can stand side by side; man will thereby find his right path of freedom between the Luciferic deviation into illusions in thought and life, and the Ahrimanic allurement into forms of the future which may satisfy his pride but cannot as yet be his present forms.

To fall into Luciferic illusions means not to become fully Man—not to wish to progress to the stage of spiritual freedom but to wish to halt, as God-Man, at a premature stage of evolution. To succumb to Ahrimanic temptations means not to be willing to wait until at a certain stage of human development the right cosmic moment will have come, but to wish to forestall this stage.

Michael-Christ will stand in future as the guiding word at the entrance to the path upon which man may arrive at his world-goal, in a way that is cosmically right, between the Luciferic and the Ahrimanic powers.

Further Leading Thoughts issued from the Goetheanum for the Anthroposophical Society (with reference to the preceding study)

115. Man goes on his way through the Cosmos in such manner that his looking back into past ages can be falsified by the impulses of Lucifer, and his thinking into the future deceived by the allurements of Ahriman.

116. To the falsifying influences of Lucifer he finds the right relation when he imbues his attitude to life and knowledge with the Being and the Mission of Michael.

117. Moreover, in so doing he provides against the allurements of Ahriman. For the path of the Spirit into external Nature, which Michael inspires, leads to a right relation to the domain of Ahriman, inasmuch as a true and living experience with Christ is also found thereby.

MICHAEL'S MISSION IN THE COSMIC AGE OF HUMAN FREEDOM

When the work of Michael at the present time is approached through spiritual experience, it becomes possible, from the spiritual-scientific point of view, to obtain light on the cosmic nature of Freedom.

This does not refer to my Philosophy of Freedom (or 'Philosophy of Spiritual Activity,') which is based on the purely human faculties of cognition, where these are operative in the field of the spirit. In order to follow the thought of this book, it is not yet necessary to join company with the beings of other worlds. But it may be said that the Philosophy of Freedom prepares the way for the understanding of the freedom which, in spiritual connection with Michael, can then be experienced. And this is as follows.

If freedom is to be a living reality in human action, then that which is accomplished in the light of it must be completely independent of man's physical and etheric organisation. There can be no freedom except through the 'I,' and the astral body must be able to vibrate in harmony with the free activity of the 'I,' so that it may be able to transmit it to the physical and etheric bodies. But this is only one side of the matter. The other side becomes clear in connection with the mission of Michael. For it is also true that what man experiences in freedom must not in any way affect his physical or etheric body. Were this to happen, he would have to lose entirely what he had gained during his evolution under the influence of Divine-Spiritual Being, and Divine-Spiritual Manifestation.

What man experiences through this his environment which is but the accomplished Work of the Divine and Spiritual, must take effect on his spiritual nature (i.e. his Ego) only. His physical and etheric organisation must only be affected by that which flows on, in the stream of evolution, not in his outer environment, but within his own being, and which had its origin in the Being and Manifestation of the Divine-Spiritual. But this must not work together with that in the human being which lives in the element of freedom.

All this is only made possible because Michael carries over from the far past of evolution something that brings man into connection with that Divine-Spiritual reality which in the present day no longer penetrates the physical and etheric organisation. Through this the foundation is being laid, within the mission of Michael, for a human intercourse with the spiritual world which does not interfere at all with the working of Nature.

It is inspiring to see how the human being is raised by Michael into the spiritual sphere, whereas the unconscious and subconscious elements which develop beneath the sphere of freedom are uniting ever more strongly with the world of matter.

Man's position with respect to the world will in the future become more and more incomprehensible to him if he is not prepared to recognise, in addition to his relations to the beings and processes of Nature, such relations as this to the Michael Mission. Our relations to Nature are recognised by looking at them from without; our relations to the spiritual world proceed from something like an inner conversation with Beings to whom we have opened up the way by adopting a spiritual view of the world.

In order, therefore, for man to realise the impulse of freedom, he must be able to hold at a distance certain influences of Nature which affect his being from the Cosmos. This 'holding at a distance' is taking place in the subconsciousness, when in the consciousness there are the forces which represent the life of the Ego in freedom. For the inward perception of man himself there is the consciousness of his activity in freedom, but for the spiritual Beings connected with man from other spheres of the Universe it is different. The Being from the hierarchy of the Angeloi, who leads human existence from one earthly life to another, sees at once how the matter stands regarding human action in freedom; he sees how man thrusts away from himself cosmic forces which want to form and mould him further—which want to give to his Ego-organisation the necessary physical supports, as they did before the age of Michael.

Michael, who is a member of the hierarchy of the Arch-angeloi, receives his impressions with the aid of the Beings of the Angeloi-hierarchy. He devotes himself, in the manner here described, to the task of bringing to man from the spiritual part of the Cosmos forces which can replace those from the realm of Nature which have been suppressed.

He accomplishes this by bringing his activity into the most perfect accord with the Mystery of Golgotha.

The forces which man requires for the compensation of suppressed impulses of Nature when he acts through freedom, are contained in the activity of Christ within earthly evolution. But man must then really bring his soul into that inner life in union with Christ, of which we have already spoken in these articles on the Michael Mission.

When a man faces the physical Sun and receives from it warmth and light he knows that he is living in a reality. In the same way he must live in the presence of Christ, the spiritual Sun, who has joined His life to that of the Earth, and receive actively from Him into his soul that which in the spiritual world corresponds to warmth and light.

He will feel himself permeated by 'spiritual warmth' when he experiences the 'Christ in me.' Feeling himself thus permeated he will say to himself: 'This warmth liberates my human being from bonds of the Cosmos in which it may not remain. For me to gain my freedom the Divine-Spiritual Being of primeval times had to lead me into regions where it could not remain with me, where, however, it gave me Christ, that His forces might bestow upon me as a free human being what the Divine-Spiritual primeval Being once gave me by way of Nature, which was then also the

Spirit-way. This warmth leads me back again to the divine sources, whence I came.'

And in this feeling there will grow together in man, in inner warmth of soul, the experience in and with Christ and the experience of real and true humanity. 'Christ gives me my humanity'—that will be the fundamental feeling which will well up in the soul and pervade it. When this feeling is once there, another comes: man feels raised by Christ beyond mere earthly existence, he feels one with the starry firmament around the Earth and with all that can be recognised in this firmament as Spiritual and Divine.

It is the same with the spiritual Light. Man can feel himself fully in his true human nature by becoming aware of himself as a free individual. A certain darkening is however connected with this. The Divine-Spiritual of primeval times no longer shines. The primeval Light appears again in the Light brought by Christ to the human ego. In the life in union with Christ this blissful thought may shine like a sun through the whole soul: 'The glorious primal Divine Light is here again; it shines, although its light comes not from Nature.' And man unites himself, while in the present, with the spiritual, cosmic forces of Light belonging to that past when he was not yet a free individual. And in this Light he can find the paths which lead him aright as a human being, when in his soul he unites himself, with understanding, with the Michael Mission.

Then in the Spirit-warmth man will feel the impulse which so carries him over into his cosmic future, that in this future he will be able to remain true to the original gifts of Divine-Spiritual Beings, albeit he has evolved in their worlds to free individuality. And in the Spirit-light he will feel the power which leads him with open eyes and ever higher and wider consciousness to the world in which as a free human being he will find himself again with the Gods of his origin.

If man wishes to continue in the original existence and

keep the primal naïve Divine Goodness which held sway in him, and shrinks from the full use of freedom—it leads him, in this present world in which everything tends to develop his freedom, to Lucifer, who wishes the present world to be denied.

If man devotes himself to present existence and wishes the natural world alone to hold sway (the natural world which is accessible to the present intellect and which is neutral with respect to Goodness), if he wishes to experience the use of freedom in the intellect alone, then in this present world where evolution needs to be continued in deeper regions of the soul, while freedom rules in the upper regions—he will after all be led to Ahriman, who wishes to see the present world transformed into a Cosmos of pure intellectuality.

Certainty of soul and spirit flourishes in those regions where man feels that in the direction of the outer world his gaze rests spiritually on Michael, and in the direction towards the inner being of the soul on Christ. It is that certainty through which he will be able to traverse the cosmic path upon which he will, without losing his origin, in the future find his true perfection.

Further Leading Thoughts issued from the Goetheanum for the Anthroposophical Society

118. That action alone can be free in which no process of Nature, either within man or without him, plays an active part.

119. But there is also the other pole, the opposite aspect of this truth. Whenever the individuality of man works freely, a Nature-process is suppressed in him. In an unfree action this process of Nature would indeed be present, giving to the human being his cosmically predestined character.

120. To the man who with his own life and being really partakes in the present and future stages of World-evolution, this character is not vouchsafed by way of Nature. But it comes to him by way of the Spirit when he unites himself with Michael, whereby he also finds the way to Christ.

THE WORLD-THOUGHTS IN THE WORKING OF MICHAEL AND IN THE WORKING OF AHRIMAN

When one considers the relation of Michael to Ahriman, one may well feel impelled to ask: How are these spiritual Powers related to one another in the cosmic sense, seeing that both of them are active in the unfolding of the forces of Intellectuality?

In the past Michael unfolded the Intellectuality throughout the Cosmos. He did this as the servant of the Divine-Spiritual Powers, to whom both he himself and man owed their origin. And he wishes not to depart from this relationship to Intellectuality. When Intellectuality was loosened from the Divine-Spiritual Powers in order to find its way into the inner being of man, Michael resolved thenceforth to assume his true relationship to mankind in order that in mankind he might find his relationship to the Intellectuality. But he wanted to do all this only in the sense of the Divine-Spiritual Powers and as their servant still. For with these Powers he has been united ever since his own origin and that of men. Therefore it is his intention that Intellectuality shall flow in future through the hearts of men, but that it shall flow there as the self-same force which it was in the beginning when it poured forth from the Divine-Spiritual Powers.

It is altogether different with Ahriman. He is a Being who long, long ago severed himself from the stream of evolution to which those Divine-Spiritual Powers belong of whom we are speaking. In an age of primal antiquity he set himself up beside them as an independent power in the Cosmos. This Being, though in the present day he is there in the world of space to which man belongs, evolves no relationship of inner forces with the Beings rightly belonging to this world. It is only through the Intellectuality, loosened from the Divine-Spiritual Beings, which comes into this world, that Ahriman —finding himself akin to it—is able in his own way to unite himself with mankind. For in an ancient and primeval past he already united with himself this Intellectuality which man receives in the present as a gift from the Cosmos. Ahriman, if he succeeded in his intentions, would make the intellect, given to mankind, similar to his own.

Now Ahriman appropriated Intellectuality to himself in an age when he could not make it an inner reality within him. It has remained in his being as a force, utterly detached from anything of heart or soul. Intellectuality pours forth from Ahriman as a cold and freezing, soulless cosmic impulse. Those human beings who are taken hold of by this impulse bring forth that logic which seems to speak for itself alone, void of compassion and of love, which bears no evidence of a right, heartfelt, inner relationship of soul between the human being and what he thinks and speaks and does. In real truth it is Ahriman who speaks in this kind of logic.

But Michael has never appropriated Intellectuality to himself. He rules it as a Divine-Spiritual force while feeling himself united with the Divine-Spiritual Powers. And when *he* pervades the intellect it becomes manifest that the intellect can equally well be an expression of the heart and soul as an expression of the head and mind. For Michael has within him all the original forces of his Gods as well as those of man. Consequently he does not convey to the intellect anything that is soulless, cold, frosty, but he stands by it in a manner that is full of soul and inwardly warm.

Herein, too, lies the reason why Michael moves through the Cosmos with earnest mien and gesture. To be inwardly united in this way with intelligence means at the same time to be obliged to fulfil the requirement that into it shall be brought no subjective caprice, wish or desire. Otherwise logic becomes the arbitrary activity of *one* being, instead of the expression of the Cosmos. Michael considers that *his* special virtue consists in strictly maintaining his being as the expression of the World-Being, keeping within himself all that would make itself felt as his own being. His aims are directed towards the great purposes of the Cosmos; this is expressed in his mien. His will, as it approaches man, must reflect what he sees in the Cosmos; and this is shown in his attitude, his gesture. Michael is *earnest* in all things, for earnestness, as the manifestation of a being, is a reflection of the Cosmos from this being; smiling is the expression of that which proceeds and radiates from a being into the world.

One of the Imaginations of Michael is the following: he rules through the passage of time; bearing the light from the Cosmos really as his own being; giving form to the warmth from the Cosmos as the revealer of his own being; as a being he keeps steadily on his course like a world, affirming himself only by affirming the world, as if leading forces down to the Earth from all parts of the Universe.

Contrast this with an Imagination of Ahriman: As he goes along he would like to capture space from time; he has darkness around him into which he shoots the rays of his own light; the more he achieves his aims the severer is the frost around him; he moves as a world which contracts entirely into one being, viz., his own, in which he affirms himself only by denying the world; he moves as if he carried with him the sinister forces of dark caves in the Earth.

When man seeks freedom without inclining towards egoism—when freedom becomes for him pure love for the action which is to be performed—then it is possible for him to approach Michael. But if he desires to act freely and at the same time develops egoism—if freedom becomes for him the proud feeling of manifesting *himself* in the action—then he is in danger of falling into Ahriman's sphere.

The Imaginations we have just described shine forth from a man's pure love for the action (Michael), or from his own self-love in acting (Ahriman).

When man feels himself as a free being in proximity to Michael he is on the way to carry the intellectual power into his 'whole man'; he thinks indeed with his head, but his heart feels the brightness of the thought or its shade; the will radiates forth the essential being of man by allowing thoughts to stream into it as intentions and aims. Man becomes more and more man by becoming the expression of the world; he finds himself, not by *seeking* himself, but by uniting himself voluntarily with the world.

If, when man unfolds his freedom, he succumbs to Ahriman's temptations, he is drawn into intellectuality as if into a spiritual automatic process in which he is a part; he is no longer himself. All his thinking becomes an experience of the head; but this separates it from the experience of his own heart and the life of his own will, and blots out his own being. Man loses more and more of the true inner human expression by becoming the expression of his own separate existence; he loses himself by *seeking* himself, he withdraws himself from the world which he refuses to love. It is only when he loves the world that a man truly experiences himself.

From the above description it may be evident that Michael is the Guide to Christ. Michael goes with love on his way through the world, with all the earnestness of his nature, attitude and action. The man who attaches himself to him cultivates love *in relation to the outer world.* And love must be unfolded first of all in relation to the outer world, otherwise it becomes self-love.

If this love in the spirit of Michael is there, then one's love of another being will shine back into one's own self. The self will be able to love without loving itself. And on the paths of this love Christ can be found by the human soul.

One who holds fast to Michael cultivates love in relation to the outer world, and he thereby finds that relation to the inner world of his soul which brings him in touch with Christ.

The age now dawning requires that humanity should turn its attention to a world immediately bordering upon the world perceived as physical—one in which can be found what we have here described as the Being and the Mission of Michael. For the world which man pictures as Nature when he sees this physical world, is also not the one in which he is immediately living, but one which lies as far *below* the truly human world as the world of Michael lies *above* it. It is only that man fails to notice that unconsciously, when he makes for himself a picture of his world, the image of another world really arises. When he paints this picture he at the same time excludes himself and succumbs to the spiritual automatic process. Man can only preserve his humanity by placing over against *this* picture, in which he loses himself in the picture of Nature, the other, in which Michael rules—in which Michael leads the way to Christ.

Further Leading Thoughts issued from the Goetheanum for the Anthroposophical Society (in connection with the foregoing account of the World-Thoughts in the Working of Michael and in the Working of Ahriman)

121. We have not fully understood the significance for the Universe of something that is working there—for instance, of the Cosmic Thoughts—so long as we stop short at the thing itself. We must also look to recognise the Beings from whom it proceeds. Thus for the Cosmic Thoughts we must see whether it is Michael or Ahriman who bears them out into the world and through the world.

122. Proceeding from the one Being—by virtue of his relation to the world—the same thing will work creatively and wholesomely; proceeding from another, it will prove fatal and destructive. The Cosmic Thoughts carry man into the future when he receives them from Michael; they lead him away from the future of his salvation when Ahriman has power to give them to him.

123. Such reflections lead us ever more to overcome the idea of an undefined Spirituality, pantheistically conceived as holding sway at the root of all things. We are led to a

conception that is definite and real, capable of clear ideas about the spiritual Beings of the Hierarchies. For the reality is everywhere a reality of Being. Whatsoever in it is not Being, is the activity that proceeds in the relation of one Being to another. This too can only be understood if we can turn our gaze to the active Beings.

FIRST STUDY: AT THE GATES OF THE SPIRITUAL SOUL (CONSCIOUSNESS-SOUL). HOW MICHAEL IN THE SPIRITUAL WORLD IS PREPARING FOR HIS EARTH-MISSION THROUGH THE CONQUEST OF LUCIFER

A clear light is thrown upon the entrance of Michael into the evolution of the world and humanity at the end of the nineteenth century, by a study of the spiritual history of the preceding centuries.

The epoch of the Spiritual Soul takes its rise at the beginning of the fifteenth century.

Before this time a complete change is taking place in the spiritual life of mankind. It is evident on looking back, that Imaginations still play a large part in human perception. Single individuals, it is true, have already associated themselves in their soul-life with pure 'concepts'; but the soul-life of the greater number of people consists in a struggle between Imaginations on the one hand, and ideas born from the purely physical world on the other. This is true, not only as regards ideas concerning events in the world of Nature, but also those concerning the developments of history.

What spiritual observation is able to discover in this direction is confirmed throughout by external evidence. Let us now look at some instances of this.

The way in which people in previous centuries had thought and spoken about historical events had found its way into writing just before the age of the Spiritual Soul set in. Thus we have preserved to us out of this time 'sagas' and the like, in which a true picture is given of how 'history' was represented in past times.

A fine example is the story of 'Gerhard the Good,' contained in a poem by Rudolf of Ems, who lived in the first half of the thirteenth century. 'Gerhard the Good' is a rich merchant of Cologne. He undertakes a journey to Russia, Livonia and Prussia, to buy sables, and then travels farther to Damascus and Nineveh to get silk-stuffs and similar merchandise.

On the homeward journey he is driven out of his course by a storm. In the strange country in which he finds himself he becomes acquainted with a man, who is keeping a number of English knights, and the betrothed of the King of England, in captivity. Gerhard sacrifices all that he has acquired on his journey by trading, and receives the prisoners in exchange. When the ships arrive at the point where the ways of the travellers part, Gerhard sends the knights home, but the King's betrothed he detains, in the hope that the bridegroom, King William, will come to fetch her himself, as soon as he receives news of her release, and of the place of her abode. The King's bride and the maidens who accompany her are entertained by Gerhard in the best way imaginable. She lives, like a much loved daughter, in the house of her deliverer from captivity. A long time passes without the King coming to take her away. Then, in order to ensure his foster-daughter's future, Gerhard decides to marry her to his son. For the supposition is possible that William is dead. The wedding of Gerhard's son is being celebrated, when an unknown pilgrim arrives. It is William. He has wandered about for a long time, searching for his betrothed. Gerhard's son unselfishly resigns her and she is given back to William. Both remain for a time with Gerhard; then the latter fits out a ship to convey them to England. When Gerhard's prisoners—who have been restored to honour—are first able to greet him in England they wish to make him king. But he is able to reply that he is bringing to them their lawful king and queen. They, too, had thought William dead and wished to choose another king to rule their country, which during William's wanderings had fallen into a chaotic state. The Cologne merchant renounces all the honours and riches offered to him and returns to Cologne, there to be again the simple merchant he had been before. The story goes on to relate how Otto I, King of Saxony, journeys to Cologne to make the acquaintance of Gerhard the Good. For the powerful king has succumbed to the temptation to count upon 'earthly recompense' for much that he has done. Through becoming acquainted with Gerhard he learns from his example how a simple man does an unspeakable amount of good—sacrificing all the goods he had acquired in order to liberate captives; restoring to William his son's affianced bride; then taking the trouble to convey William to England again, etc.—without desiring any earthly reward whatever for it, but leaving all reward to the ruling of Divine Providence. The man is universally known as 'Gerhard the Good'; the king feels that he himself receives a strong moral and religious impulse through becoming acquainted with Gerhard's mind and character.

The story which I have briefly outlined above—in order not merely to indicate by name something that is little known—shows quite clearly *from one aspect* the mental attitude of the age before the coming of the Spiritual Soul in the evolution of humanity.

Those who enter into the spirit of the story, as told by Rudolf of Ems, will be able to feel how the experience of the earthly world has changed since the time of King Otto (the tenth century).

Notice how, during the age of the Spiritual Soul, the world has in a certain way become 'clear' to the mental eye of man, as regards the comprehension of physical existence and its development. Gerhard travels with his ships as if in a mist. He only knows the small portion of the world with which he wishes to come in contact. In Cologne you hear nothing of what is taking place in England, and you have to search for years for a person who is in Cologne. You get to know about the life and property of another man such as the one on whose shore Gerhard is cast on his homeward journey, only when you have been brought directly by destiny to the place. The present-day grasp of circumstances in the world is related to that of those earlier times as the looking into a broad, sunlit landscape is to the groping about in a dense fog.

What is related in connection with Gerhard the Good has nothing to do with what we call 'historical' now-a-days, but it is all the more concerned with the character and mood of soul and with the whole spiritual situation of the time. It is these, and not the single events in the physical world, which are depicted in Imaginations.

In the picture before us, we see a reflection of how man not only feels himself as a being who lives and is active as a member in the chain of events in the physical world, but also feels spiritual, supersensible Beings working into his earthly existence and having connection with his will.

The tale of Gerhard the Good shows how the twilight-dimness, which, in respect of the penetration of the physical world, preceded the period of the Spiritual Soul, turned man's gaze to the vision of the spiritual world. Man did not see the *breadth* of the physical world, but he saw all the more into the *depth* of the spiritual.

Yet in the period that we describe, it was no longer the same as it once had been when a twilight clairvoyance showed to mankind the spiritual world. The Imaginations were there; but when they appeared within the human soul, it was already in its apprehension of things strongly disposed in the direction of thought. The result of this was that men no longer knew how the world that revealed itself in Imaginations was related to the world of physical existence. Hence, to people who were already holding more strongly to the thought element, these Imaginations seemed to be fictions, invented at will and having no reality.

Men no longer knew that through the Imaginations they saw into a world in which man stands with a quite different part of his being than in the physical world. Thus in the picture before us, two worlds stand side by side; and in the way the story is told, both worlds bear a character that would make one believe the spiritual events to have taken place in among the physical events, and just as perceptibly as these.

In addition to this, the physical events in many of these tales are in utter confusion. People whose lives are centuries apart appear as contemporaries; events are transferred to another place or period.

Facts of the physical world are viewed by the human soul in such a way as one can really only view what is spiritual, for which Time and Space have a different significance. The physical world is depicted in Imaginations instead of in thoughts. On the other hand, the spiritual world is woven into the narrative as if one were dealing, not with a different form of existence, but with something that was a continuation of physical facts.

A historical conception that keeps to the physical only, thinks that the old Imaginations of the East, of Greece, etc., have been taken over and interwoven poetically with the historical subjects that were occupying men's minds at the time. The writings of Isidor of Seville of the seventh century are said to contain a regular collection of old legendary 'motifs.'

Yet this is merely an external point of view, and has significance only for those who have no understanding of that condition of soul which still knows itself to be in direct connection with the spiritual world, and which feels itself impelled to express this knowledge in Imaginations. Whether a writer makes use of his own Imagination, or whether he applies, in an understanding and living way, one that has been handed down through history, is not the essential point. The essential point is that the soul is orientated towards the spiritual world and sees both its own actions and the events in the course of Nature as forming a part of that world.

It is however true that in the way stories and legends were told in the time before the dawn of the epoch of the Spiritual Soul, a certain tendency to error is noticeable.

Spiritual observation sees in this tendency the working of the Luciferic powers.

That which urges the soul to receive the Imaginations into its experience is the result not so much of faculties possessed by the soul in ancient times—through a dreamlike clairvoyance—but rather of faculties present in the periods between the eighth and the fourteenth centuries A.D. These faculties were already pressing more strongly towards an understanding, in terms of thought, of what was perceived by the senses. Both kinds of faculties were present simultaneously during the transition period. The soul was placed between the old orientation, which penetrates to the spiritual world and sees the physical only as in a mist, and the new orientation, which is centred on physical happenings and in which the spiritual vision fades.

The Luciferic power works into this wavering balance of the human soul. It wants to prevent man from attaining to complete orientation in the physical world. It wants to keep him, with his consciousness, in spiritual realms that were adapted for him in ancient times. It wants to prevent pure thinking, directed towards the understanding of physical existence, from flowing into his dreamlike, imaginative conception of the world. It is able to hold back, in a wrong way, man's power of perception from the physical world. It is not however, able to maintain in the right way the experience of the old Imaginations, And so it makes man reflect imaginatively, and yet at the same time he is not able to transplant his soul completely into the world in which the Imaginations have their full value.

At the dawn of the Spiritual Soul epoch, Lucifer is active in such a manner that, through him, man is transplanted to the supersensible region immediately bordering on the physical in a way not in keeping with his nature.

We can see this quite clearly in the legend of Duke Ernst (Herzog Ernst), which was one of the favourite legends of the Middle Ages and was related in wide circles.

Duke Ernst has a disagreement with the Emperor, who is determined to make war upon him unjustly and bring him to ruin. The Duke feels impelled to escape from this untenable relation with the head of the State by taking part in the Crusade to the East. In the experiences which he goes through before he reaches his destination, the physical and spiritual are woven together in saga form in the manner indicated. For instance, the Duke, in the course of his wanderings, encounters a people with heads shaped like those of cranes. He is driven ashore on the Magnet Mountain, which draws ships with magnetic power, so that people who come into the vicinity of the mountain cannot escape, but are doomed to a miserable end. Duke Ernst and his followers effect their escape by sewing themselves up in skins, and letting themselves be carried on to a hill by griffins, who are accustomed to capture those driven on to the Magnet Mountain; thence, after cutting the skins, they escape in the absence of the griffins. The continuation of the journey leads them to a people whose ears are so long that they can fling them round them like a cloak; and to yet another people whose feet are so large that when it rains, they can lie on the ground and spread their feet over them like umbrellas.

He comes from a race of dwarfs to a race of giants, etc. Many similar things are related in connection with the Duke Ernst's journey to the Crusades. The 'Legend' does not let one feel in the right way how, whenever Imaginations enter into the story, an orientation is set up towards a spiritual world, and how events are then related through pictures which are enacted in the astral world, and which are connected with the Will and Fate of earthly man.

This is also the case with the beautiful 'Story of Roland,' in which Charles the Great's crusade against the heathen in Spain is commemorated. It is related there (as if in confirmation of the Bible) that in order that Charles the Great could attain the end he was striving for, the sun stopped in its course, so that one day became as long as two.

In the case of the 'Nibelung Saga,' one can see how in Northern lands it has kept a form that maintains more purely and directly the perception of the Spiritual, whereas in Central Europe the Imaginations are brought nearer to physical life. In the Northern form of the story the Imaginations are referred to an 'astral world'; in the Central European form of the Lay of the Nibelungs, the Imaginations glide over into the perception of the physical world.

The Imaginations appearing in the Legend of Duke Ernst refer in reality to what is experienced *between* the experiences in the physical sphere, in an 'astral world,' to which man belongs just as much as to the physical.

If one applies spiritual vision to all this, then one sees how the entrance into the Age of Consciousness signifies outgrowing a phase of evolution in which the Luciferic powers would have prevailed over mankind, had not a new evolutionary impulse come into the human being through the Spiritual Soul with its force of intellectuality. That orientation towards the spiritual world which would lead into the paths of error is hindered through the Spiritual Soul; the gaze of man is drawn away and turned upon the physical world. Everything that happens in this direction withdraws humanity from the Luciferic powers that are misleading it.

Michael is already at this time active for humanity from the spiritual world. He is preparing his later work from out of the supersensible. He is giving humanity impulses which preserve the former relation to the Divine-Spiritual world, without this preservation adopting a Luciferic character.

Then in the last third of the nineteenth century Michael himself presses forward into the physical earthly world with the activities which he has exercised in preparation from out of the Supersensible, from the fifteenth to the nineteenth century.

Humanity had to undergo a period of spiritual evolution for the purpose of freeing itself from that relation to the spiritual world which threatened to become an impossible one. Then the evolution was guided, through the Michael Mission, into paths which brought the progress of Earth-humanity once more into a good and healthy relation to the spiritual world.

Thus Michael stands in his activity between the Luciferic *World-picture*, and the Ahrimanic *World-intellect*. The World-picture becomes through him a *World-revelation* full of wisdom, which reveals the World-intellect as Divine *World-activity*. And in this World-activity lives the care of Christ for humanity—even in the World-activity which can thus reveal itself to the heart of man out of Michael's World-revelation.

Further Leading Thoughts issued from the Goetheanum for the Anthroposophical Society (in connection with the above study of Michael's supersensible preparation for his earthly mission)

124. The dawn of the age of Consciousness (the age of the Spiritual Soul) in the fifteenth century was preceded, in the twilight of the age of the Intellectual or Mind-Soul, by a heightened Luciferian activity, which continued for a certain time even into the new epoch.

125. This Luciferian influence tried to preserve ancient forms of pictorial conception of the world in a wrong way. Thus it tried to prevent man from understanding with Intellectuality and entering with fullness of life into the physical existence of the World.

126. Michael unites his being with the activity of mankind so that the independent Intellectuality may remain—not in a Luciferian, but in a righteous way—with the Divine and Spiritual from which it is inherited.

SECOND STUDY: HOW THE MICHAEL FORCES WORK IN THE EARLIEST UNFOLDING OF THE SPIRITUAL SOUL

At the time when the Spiritual Soul was entering the evolution of mankind on Earth, it was difficult for the Beings of the spiritual world next to this earthly existence to approach mankind. The form assumed by earthly events at that time proves that very peculiar conditions were necessary in order to enable the Spirit to find its way into the physical life of mankind. But it shows another thing as well, and in a way that is often most illuminating. It shows how, at a point when the Powers of the past are still at work and those of the future already beginning their activity, one spiritual influence tries to find its way into the earthly life of mankind in vigorous opposition to another.

Between 1339 and 1453 a chaotic, devastating war begins between France and England. It lasts for more than a hundred years. In the chaos of this war, which was due to a certain spiritual current unfavourable to the evolution of mankind, events which would otherwise have brought the Spiritual Soul into humanity more quickly were definitely hindered. Chaucer, who died in 1400, laid the foundations of English literature. We need only remember the great spiritual consequences which took their start in Europe from the founding of this literature, and we shall see the importance of the fact that such an event was not able to work itself out freely, but fell into the midst of the confusions of a prolonged war. Moreover, already in 1215 that way of political thought which can receive its true stamp and character through the Spiritual Soul had begun in England. The further evolution of this fact, too, fell into all the hindrances of war.

This was a time when the spiritual forces, seeking to evolve man according to the potentialities laid in him from the very beginning by yet loftier Divine-Spiritual Powers, encountered their strong adversaries. These adversaries wish to divert man into channels other than those appointed for him from the beginning. If they were to succeed, man would not be able to apply the forces of his origin to his further evolution. His cosmic childhood would remain unfruitful for him. It would become a dying, withering part within his being. The consequence would be that man could then fall a prey to the Luciferic or Ahrimanic Powers and lose his own true and proper development. If the adversaries of mankind had succeeded in their efforts—if they had not only put hindrances in the way, but achieved complete success—the entry of the Spiritual Soul could have been prevented.

An event which reveals the inpouring of the Spiritual into the earthly events in a most clear and radiant way is the appearance and subsequent history of Joan of Arc, the Maid of Orleans (1412–1431). The impulses for what she does lie in the deep, subconscious foundations of her soul. She follows dim inspirations from the spiritual world. On the Earth there is confusion and disorder, through which the age of the Spiritual Soul is to be hindered. Michael has to prepare from the spiritual world his later mission; this he is able to do where his impulses are received into human souls. Such a soul lives in the Maid of Orleans. And Michael also worked through many other souls, although this was possible only in a minor degree and is less apparent in outer historical life. In events such as the war between England and France he met with opposition from his Ahrimanic adversary.

In our last number we spoke of the Luciferic adversary Michael found at the same time. And indeed, this adversary is particularly apparent in the course of events following upon the appearance of the Maid of Orleans. From these events it may be seen that mankind no longer knew how to deal with an intervention of the spiritual world in the destiny of humanity, which could be understood and also received by men into the will as long as Imaginative understanding existed. The earlier attitude towards such intervention became impossible when the Intellectual Soul ceased to act; the attitude corresponding to the Spiritual Soul had not at that time been discovered; nor has it yet been achieved.

Thus it came about that Europe was moulded from the spiritual world without men understanding what was happening, and without that which they were able to do having any appreciable influence on this process.

The significance of this event, the determining causes of which lay in the spiritual world, will be perceived if one tries to imagine what would have happened in the fifteenth century had there been no Maid of Orleans. There are some who wish to explain this phenomenon materialistically. It is impossible to come to an understanding with such people because they arbitrarily interpret in the materialistic sense something that is obviously spiritual.

In certain directions of spiritual striving, too, it may now be clearly seen that humanity can no longer find the way to the Divine-Spiritual without difficulty, even though men search with resolution. There are difficulties which did not exist in the age when insight could still be gained with the aid of Imaginations. In order to judge correctly what is here meant, all that is necessary is to see in a clear light those individuals who come forward as philosophical thinkers. A philosopher cannot be judged by his effect on his age alone, nor by observing how many people have accepted his ideas. He is rather the *expression*, the manifestation in person for his age. The philosopher presents in his ideas that which the greater part of humanity bears within it as its frame of mind, unconscious feelings and impulses of life. Like a thermometer which registers the degree of the surrounding warmth, he registers the mental condition of his age. The philosophers are no more the causes of the psychology of their age than the thermometer is the cause of the surrounding temperature.

Consider, from this point of view, the philosopher René Descartes, who worked when the age of the Spiritual Soul had already commenced. (He lived from 1596 to 1650.) The slender support for his connection with the spirit-world (the world of true being) is the experience 'I think, therefore I am.' In the centre of self-consciousness, in the 'I,' he tries to feel reality; and indeed, only so much as the Spiritual Soul can tell him.

And he endeavours intellectually to understand the rest of the Spiritual by inquiring what guarantee the certainty of his own self-consciousness gives for the certainty of anything else. Regarding the truths handed on to him historically he always inquires: Are they as clear as the 'I think, therefore I am'? And if he can answer this in the affirmative he accepts them.

In this kind of human thought is not the Spirit eliminated from all observation that is directed towards the things in the world? The manifestation of the Spirit has withdrawn to the pin-point support in self-consciousness; all else, as it shows itself *directly*, is void of any revelation of the Spirit. Only indirectly, by the intellect in the Spiritual Soul, can the light of this spirit-revelation be thrown on that which lies outside self-consciousness. The man of this age allows the content of his Spiritual Soul, which is as yet almost empty, to stream towards the spiritual world with intense longing. A tiny ray goes thither.

The beings in the Spirit-world immediately bordering upon the Earth-world, and the human souls on Earth, come to one another with difficulty. Michael's supersensible preparation for his later Mission is also experienced by the human soul only under the greatest hindrances.

In order to grasp the essential nature of the frame of mind expressed in Descartes, compare this philosopher with St. Augustine, who, in the outer formulation of it, sets up for the experience of the spiritual world the same support as Descartes. But in St. Augustine it takes place out of the full force of the Intellectual or Mind-Soul. St. Augustine (354–430) is justly found to be related to Descartes, but his intellect is still the remnant of what is cosmic, whereas that of Descartes is the intellect that is already entering the individual human soul. In the progress of spiritual striving from St. Augustine to Descartes it may be seen how the cosmic character of the power of thought is lost and how it then reappears in the human soul. But it can also be seen at the same time with what difficulty Michael and the human soul come together so that Michael may lead in man what he once led in the Cosmos.

The Luciferic and Ahrimanic forces are at work to prevent this union. The Luciferic forces want man to unfold only that which was proper to him during his cosmic childhood; the Ahrimanic forces, which are opposed to the Luciferic and yet co-operate with them, would like to develop only those forces which were gained in later ages of the world, and so let the cosmic childhood of man wither away.

Under increased resistances such as these, the human souls in Europe digested the spiritual impulses contained in old world-conceptions which had streamed from the East to the West through the Crusades. The Michael-forces lived very strongly in these conceptions. The Cosmic Intelligence, the rulership of which was the ancient spiritual heritage of Michael, was dominant in these old world-conceptions.

How could they be received, seeing that there was a chasm between the forces of the spirit-world and the human souls? These forces came to the Spiritual Soul which was only just beginning to evolve. On one side they met with the hindrance given in the Spiritual Soul itself which was still but little developed. And on the other they no longer found a consciousness supported by Imagination. The human soul could not with full insight unite them with itself. They were accepted either quite superficially or superstitiously.

We have to pay attention to this frame of mind if we wish to understand the movements of thought connected on the one hand with the names of Wycliffe, Huss and others, and on the other with the name of 'Rosicrucianism.'

Further Leading Thoughts issued from the Goetheanum for the Anthroposophical Society (in connection with the foregoing Second Study of the Michael Forces in the earliest Unfolding of the Spiritual Soul)

127. At the beginning of the Age of Consciousness, man evolved the intellectual forces of his soul only to a small extent as yet. Hence there arose a gap between what the soul of man in unconscious depths was longing for, and what the forces from the region of Michael's abode could give him.

128. Owing to this gap, there was a greater possibility for the Luciferic powers to hold man back in the forces of cosmic childhood, thus bringing about his further evolution, not on the paths of the Divine-Spiritual Powers with whom he was united from the beginning, but on the paths of Lucifer.

129. Moreover there was a greater possibility for the powers of Ahriman to wrest man away from the forces of his cosmic childhood, thus dragging him down, for his further evolution, into their own domain.

130. Neither of these dangers was realised, for the forces of Michael were after all at work. But the spiritual evolution of mankind had to take place under the resulting hindrances, and it was thus that it became what it has, in fact, hitherto become.

SECOND STUDY (CONTINUED). HINDRANCES AND HELPS TO THE MICHAEL FORCES IN THE DAWN OF THE AGE OF THE SPIRITUAL SOUL

Throughout Europe, the incorporation of the Spiritual Soul brought about a disturbance in the experiences of religious faith and ritual. A clear sign of the coming disturbance may be seen about the turn of the eleventh and twelfth centuries in the arising of the 'Proofs of God' (especially in the work of Anselm of Canterbury). The existence of God now had to be proved by intellectual reasoning. The desire to do such a thing could only arise when the old way of experiencing 'God' with the forces of the inner soul was vanishing. For we never set out to prove by logic what we experience in such a way.

The old way was to perceive with one's inner soul the Beings or Intelligences, up to the Godhead. The new way, arising at this time, was to evolve intellectual thoughts about the Prime Foundations of the Universe. The former way was supported by the forces of Michael in the spiritual realm of Earth. Behind the thought-forces directed to the things of outer sense, the forces of Michael equipped the soul with faculties to perceive divine Being and Intelligence in the Universe. On the other hand, for the second way to find its fulfilment, the inner union of the soul with the forces of Michael must first be developed and accomplished.

In the sphere of religious ritual, even the central doctrine of the Holy Communion began to totter. We find this happening in far-spread regions of the religious experience of man, from Wycliffe in England (fifteenth century) to Huss in Bohemia.

In Holy Communion man was able to find his union with the spiritual world which was opened up to him through Christ. For he was able to unite his being with Christ in such a way that the fact of the outer sense-union was at the same time a spiritual fact.

The consciousness of the Intellectual or Mind-Soul was

able to form an idea of this union. For the Mind-Soul still possessed ideas, both of Spirit and of Matter, near to one another—so that it was possible for it to conceive the one (Matter) passing over into the other (Spirit). Ideas of this kind, however, cannot possibly be so intellectualistic as to require at the same time proofs of God's existence. Such ideas must still contain something of the living Imagination which enables man to feel, in Matter, the Spirit that is active in it; and in the Spirit, the striving towards Matter. Ideas of this kind have the cosmic forces of Michael behind them.

Think only how much was beginning to totter for the human soul at that time: how much of what was connected with the innermost and holiest experience of men! Personalities arose—Huss, Wycliffe and others—in whom the existence of the Spiritual Soul shone out most radiantly. Their inner state of soul was such as to unite them with the Michael forces with an intensity that would not come for others till centuries afterwards. From the voice of Michael in their hearts, they proclaimed the worthiness of the Spiritual Soul to rise to the conception of the deepest religious mysteries. They felt that the Intellectuality which was coming with the Spiritual Soul must be able to include in the realm of its ideas that which had been attainable, in older times, by Imagination.

On the other hand, the historical and traditional attitude of the human soul to these things had in very wide circles lost all its inner force and strength. What history refers to as the evils and abuses of religious life which were dealt with by the great Councils of Reform in the age when the Spiritual Soul was beginning its activity—all this is connected with the life of those human souls who, not yet feeling the Spiritual Soul within them, were on the other hand no longer able to find in the old Intellectual or Mind-Soul a sufficient source of inner strength or certainty.

Historical experiences of men, such as were laid bare at the Councils of Constance and Basle, may be said to reveal:—in the spiritual world above the downpouring of the Intellectuality seeking to find its way to men, and in the earthly realm below, the working of the Intellectual or Mind-Soul, no longer in accordance with the time. The Michael forces are hovering between, looking back to their own past union with the Divine-Spiritual, and down upon the human realm. The human realm likewise enjoyed the same union in the past, but it must now pass into a sphere in which Michael will help it from the Spirit, though he may not unite his own inner being with this realm. Absolutely necessary as it is in cosmic evolution—yet signifying, to begin with, a disturbance in the balance of the Cosmos—this striving of Michael underlies that which mankind had to experience in that age even with respect to the most sacred truths.

We gaze deeply into the characteristic features of that age when we turn our thoughts to Cardinal Nicholas of Cusa. (One may read what I have said about him in the book 'Mysticism at the Dawn of Modern Spiritual Life . . .*') His personality is like an outstanding monument of time. He wants the affairs of the world directed by points of view, which—instead of fighting the abuses and evils of the physical world by revolutionary tendencies—meet them with healthy common-sense, seeking to restore to the proper channel those things which have become diverted from it. We recognise this tendency in the influence he brought to bear at the Council of Basle, and generally within his ecclesiastical community.

Thus Nicholas of Cusa is fully inclined towards the great change in evolution which comes with the unfolding of the Spiritual Soul. On the other hand he brings forth thoughts and ideas which reveal in a most radiant way the working of Michael's forces within them. Into the midst of his age he places the good old ideas which, in the epoch when Michael still ruled the Cosmic Intellectuality, led the human soul to the unfolding of faculties to perceive the Beings and Intelli-

* *Mysticism and Modern Thought.*

gences in the Cosmos. The 'Learned Ignorance' of which he speaks is a perception over and above that which is directed to the outer world of sense—a perception which leads man's thinking beyond the intellectuality of ordinary knowledge into a region where, in ignorance or emptiness of knowledge, the Spiritual is taken hold of by a pure, inner experience of seership.

Thus Nicholas of Cusa is a personality who, feeling in his own soul-life the disturbance of the cosmic balance by Michael, would like intuitively to contribute as much as possible towards the turning of this disturbance to the welfare of humanity.

Between the things of the spiritual life that came to light in this way there lived something else which remained hidden. Certain individuals who perceived and understood the position of the Michael-forces in the Universe, wished to prepare the forces of their own souls in such a way that they might consciously enter the spirit-realm bordering upon the earthly sphere—the realm in which Michael makes his efforts on behalf of humanity.

They sought justification for this spiritual enterprise by conducting themselves outwardly in life, in their calling and in other circumstances, in such a way that their life could not be distinguished from that of other men. By lovingly performing their earthly duties in the ordinary sense they were able to turn their inner manhood freely towards the Spiritual which we have described. What they did in this direction was something between themselves and that with which they united themselves 'in secret.' As regards what took place in the physical realm, the world was at first apparently quite unaffected by this spiritual striving. And yet all this was needed in order to bring souls into the necessary union with the Michael-world. It was not a question of 'Secret Societies' in any bad sense, nor of anything that tried to hide because it feared the light of day, but rather of persons coming together, and in so doing convincing themselves that each one in their circle possessed the true consciousness of the Michael Mission. Those who thus worked together did not speak of their work before others who through lack of understanding could only have disturbed the aims they had set themselves. These aims consisted primarily in working in spiritual streams which flow, not within earthly life, but in the spirit-world next to it, but which nevertheless cast their impulses into earthly life.

This gives an indication of the spirit-work of human beings who indeed live in the physical world but co-operate with Beings who belong to the spirit-world—Beings who do not themselves enter the physical world or incarnate in it. We are here speaking of those who, with very little reference to the real facts, are named in the world as the 'Rosicrucians.' True Rosicrucianism lies absolutely in the line of activity of the Michael Mission. It helped Michael to prepare on Earth the spirit-work which he wished to prepare for a later age.

We shall be able to estimate *what* could be achieved thereby if we consider the following.

The above-described difficulties, nay, impossibilities, for Michael to work into human souls, are connected with the fact that Michael himself, in his essential being, does not wish to come in contact in any way with the physical present of earthly life. He wishes to remain in the nexus of forces which existed for Spirits of his kind, and for human beings, *in the past.* Any contact with that with which, in present earthly life, man is *obliged* to come in contact—this Michael *could* only consider as a pollution of his being. Now in ordinary human life the spiritual experience of the soul works into the physical earthly life, and conversely the latter reacts upon the former. It is a reaction which expresses itself especially in man's frame of mind and in the direction of his soul towards some earthly thing. An interaction of this kind is as a rule the case—though not invariably—especially in persons engaged in public life. Hence the hindrances to Michael's work in many of the Reformers were very great.

The Rosicrucians overcame the difficulty in this direction

by keeping their external life—which consisted in their earthly duties—quite apart from their work with Michael. When Michael, together with his impulses, came in contact with what a Rosicrucian prepared in his soul for him, he found himself in no way exposed to the danger of meeting what was earthly. For, through the state of soul which he purposely cultivated, anything earthly was kept away from that which united the Rosicrucian with Michael.

In this way the true Rosicrucian striving formed *for Michael* the path here on the Earth towards *his* coming earthly Mission.

Further Leading Thoughts issued from the Goetheanum for the Anthroposophical Society (in connection with the above Study of the Hindrances and Helps to the Michael Forces in the Dawn of the Age of the Spiritual Soul)

131. In the beginning of the Age of the Spiritual Soul, the Intellectuality now emancipated in man wanted to occupy itself with the truths of religious faith and ritual. The life of the human soul was thereby brought into uncertainty and doubt. Men tried to prove by logic spiritual realities that were formerly a direct experience within the soul. They tried to understand, nay even to determine by logical deduction, the contents of sacred ritual which can only be taken hold of in spiritual Imaginations.

132. All this is connected with the fact that while Michael is determined to avoid any kind of contact with the present earthly world, which man *must* enter; yet at the same time it is still his task to guide in man the cosmic Intellectuality which he administered in ages past. Thus there arises through the Michael-forces a disturbance in the cosmic balance—albeit, a disturbance necessary for the further progress of world-evolution.

133. Michael's mission was made easier for him by certain personalities—the genuine Rosicrucians—who arranged their outward life on Earth so that it in no way interfered with their inner life of soul. They could thus develop forces within them, whereby they worked together in spiritual realms with Michael, without the danger of entangling him in present earthly happenings, which would have been impossible for him.

THIRD STUDY: MICHAEL'S SUFFERING OVER HUMAN EVOLUTION BEFORE THE TIME OF HIS EARTHLY ACTIVITY

As the new Age of Consciousness proceeds, it grows less and less possible for Michael to connect himself with the existence of mankind in general. Intellectuality has become human and is now entering humanity. From it the Imaginative conceptions, which could reveal to man the Divine Being and Intelligence in the Cosmos, are vanishing. The possibility for Michael himself to approach man begins only with the last third of the nineteenth century. Before that time it was only possible by those paths which were sought for in the true Rosicrucian sense.

With his own budding intellectuality, man looks out into Nature. He sees there a physical and etheric world, in which he himself is not contained. Through the great ideas of men such as Copernicus and Galileo, he attains a picture of the the world external to man. But he loses the picture of himself. When he gazes on himself he has no possibility of reaching any insight as to what he truly is.

In the depths of his being, that which is destined to bear and sustain his intelligence is being awakened in him. With this, his Ego becomes united. Thus man now bears a threefold nature within him: first, in his spirit-and-soul being, manifesting as physical-etheric, that which originated once upon a time, in the old Saturn and Sun epochs, and then ever and again placed him within the kingdom of the Divine-Spiritual. It is here that the Human Being and the Michael Being go together. Secondly, man bears within him his later physical and etheric nature, that which evolved in him during the Moon and Earth epochs. All this is the work and active working of the Divine-Spiritual. But the Divine-Spiritual itself is no longer living and present within it. It only becomes fully living and present once more when Christ passes through the Mystery of Golgotha. In that which is at work spiritually in the physical and etheric body of man, Christ can indeed be found.

Thirdly, man has within him that part of his soul and spirit which received *new* being in the Moon and Earth epochs. Here Michael has remained active (whereas in the part of man that is inclined towards the Moon and Earth, he has become more and more inactive.) In the former *Michael* has preserved, for man, his picture of Man and the Gods together.

He was able to do this until the dawn of the new age of Consciousness—the age of the Spiritual Soul. Then the spirit and soul of man sank down, as it were, entirely in the physical-etheric nature, in order to draw forth from there the Spiritual Soul.

Radiantly there arose in the consciousness of man what his physical and his etheric body could tell him about the physical and etheric in the world of Nature. And what his astral body and Ego had been able to tell him about himself vanished away from his vision.

In the age which now began, there arose in man the feeling that with his own insight he could no longer reach *himself*. Thus there began a *search* for knowledge of the human being. Man could no longer find satisfaction for this quest in what the present was able to provide. He went back to earlier ages of history. Humanism arose in the evolution of the spiritual life. Humanism became the object of men's striving, not because they had grasped Man in his essential nature, but because they had lost him. As long as they possessed this knowledge, Erasmus of Rotterdam and others would have worked from a trend of soul quite different from anything that Humanism could give them.

In *Faust*, Goethe discovered at a later time a figure representative of the man who had completely lost hold of his essential being.

This quest of the human being grows more and more intense as time goes on. For man has now no other alternative: he must either make himself blunt and insensitive as regards his own being, or else the longing for it must come forth as an essential element in his soul's life.

Right into the nineteenth century, the best minds in the spiritual life of Europe evolve ideas in the most varied fields and in the most different ways—ideas historical, scientific, philosophical, mystical, all of which represent the striving to find, in what has now become an intellectualistic world-conception, the *human being* himself.

Renaissance, spiritual re-birth, humanism, are striving restlessly—even tempestuously—for a spiritual element in a direction in which it is *not* to be found. And, in the direction in which it should be sought, there is impotence, illusion, bewilderment of consciousness. And yet everywhere—in Art, in Knowledge—the Michael-forces are breaking through into the human being, though not as yet into the newly-growing forces of the Spiritual Soul. It is a critical time for the spiritual life. Michael turns all his forces towards the past in cosmic evolution so that he may gain the power to hold the 'Dragon' balanced and constrained beneath his feet. It is under these mighty exertions of Michael that the great creations of the Renaissance are born. Yet they still only represent a renewal by Michael of Intellectual or Mind-Soul forces. They are not yet a working of the new soul-forces.

We can behold Michael filled with anxiety. Will he really be able to master the 'Dragon' in the long run? He perceives human beings in one region trying to gain a picture of Man out of the newly-acquired picture of Nature. He sees how they observe Nature and then seek to form a picture of Man from what they call the 'Laws of Nature.' He sees them forming their conceptions:—'This animal quality becomes more perfect, that system of organs more harmonious, and man "arises"!' But before the spirit-gaze of Michael *man* does not arise. For in effect, what is thus thought of as being harmonised, perfected, is there only in thought. No one can see it evolving in reality, for nowhere does this happen in actual fact.

And so, with these their conceptions about Man, men live in empty pictures, in illusions. They are for ever running after a picture of Man which they only imagine that they have, while in real truth there is nothing in their field of vision. 'The power of the spiritual Sun shines upon their souls. Christ Himself is working; but they are not yet able to perceive His presence. The power of the Spiritual Soul holds sway in the body; but it still will not enter into their souls.' That is approximately the inspiration one can hear of what Michael says in great anxiety. Is it possible that the forces of illusion in man will give the 'Dragon' so much power that it will be impossible for Michael to maintain the balance?

Other persons try with more inward artistic power to feel Nature at one with man. Mighty are the words in which Goethe described Winkelmann's work in a beautiful book: 'When the healthy nature of man acts as a whole, when he feels himself in the world as in a great, beautiful, majestic and worthy whole, when harmonious ease gives him pure, free delight; then would the Universe, if it were conscious of itself, shout aloud for joy, as having reached its goal, and marvel at the climax of its own development and being.' That which stimulated Lessing with fiery spirit and ensouled Herder's wide outlook on the world, rings out in these words of Goethe. And the whole of Goethe's own work is like a many-sided revelation of these his own words. In his 'Aesthetic Letters', Schiller has described an ideal human being who, in the sense described in the above words, bears the Universe within himself and realises it in social intercourse with other human beings. But whence comes *this* picture of Man? It shines like the morning sun over the Earth in spring. But it has entered into human feeling from study of the ancient Greeks. It arose in men with a strong inward Michael-impulse; but they could give form to this impulse only by turning the mind's eye to days of yore. When

Goethe wished to experience 'Man,' he felt himself in the greatest conflict with the Spiritual Soul. He sought for Man in Spinoza's philosophy; but only during his tour in Italy, when he studied the nature of Greek art, did he feel that he had a glimpse of him. He went away finally from the Spiritual Soul, which is striving upwards in Spinoza, to the Intellectual Soul or Mind-Soul which was gradually dying out. However, with his far-reaching conception of Nature he was able to carry over an infinite amount from the Intellectual Soul into the Spiritual Soul.

Michael also looks with earnestness upon this search for Man. What is in accordance with his idea is indeed entering here into the spiritual evolution of man:—it is *that* human being who once beheld the Divine Being and Intelligence when Michael still ruled it from the Cosmos. But if this were not laid hold of by the spiritualised force of the Spiritual Soul it would in the end inevitably slip away from Michael's control and come under the sway of Lucifer. The other great anxiety in Michael's life is, lest in the oscillation of the cosmic spiritual state of balance Lucifer might gain the upper hand.

Michael's preparation of his Mission for the end of the nineteenth century flows on in cosmic tragedy. Below, on the Earth, there is often the greatest satisfaction in the working out of the new picture of Nature; whereas in the region where Michael works there is a tragic feeling regarding the hindrances to the coming of the picture of Man.

Formerly Michael's austere, spiritualised love lived in the sun's rays, in the shimmering dawn, in the sparkling of the stars; this love had now acquired most strongly the note of looking down at humanity with awakening sorrow.

Michael's situation in the Cosmos became tragically difficult, but it also pressed for a solution just at the period of time which preceded his earthly mission. Men were able to keep intellectuality only in the sphere of the body and there only in the sphere of the senses. On one hand, therefore, they received into their views nothing that the senses did not tell them; Nature became the field of the revelations of the senses, considered quite materially. The forms of Nature were no longer perceived as the work of the Divine-Spiritual but as something devoid of spirit, and yet something of which it is affirmed that it brings forth that spiritual element in which man lives. On the other hand, as regards a Spirit-world, men would now accept only what the historical accounts narrated. Direct vision of the Spirit working in the past was discredited, as was the vision of the Spirit in the present.

In the soul of man there now lived only that which came from the sphere of the present, which Michael does not enter. Man was glad to stand on 'sure' ground. He believed he possessed this because in 'Nature' he sought no thoughts, in which he might have had to fear the presence of arbitrary fancies. But Michael was not glad. In his own sphere, beyond man, he had to wage war with Lucifer and Ahriman. This resulted in tragic difficulty, because Lucifer is able to approach man the more easily, the more Michael—who indeed also preserves the past—is obliged to keep himself away from man. And thus a severe battle *for man* took place between Michael and Ahriman and Lucifer in the spiritual world immediately bordering upon the Earth, while on the Earth itself man kept his soul in action against what was beneficial to his evolution.

All this applies of course to the spiritual life of Europe and America. We should have to speak differently with respect to that of Asia.

Further Leading Thoughts issued from the Goetheanum for the Anthroposophical Society (in connection with the above Third Study: Michael's suffering over Human Evolution before the Time of his earthly Activity)

134. In the very earliest time of the evolution of the Spiritual Soul, man began to feel that he had lost the picture of Humanity—the picture of his own Being—which had formerly been given to him in Imagination. Powerless as yet to find it in the Spiritual Soul, he sought for it by way of Natural Science or of History. He wanted the ancient picture of Humanity to arise in him again.

135. Man reaches no fulfilment in this way. Far from becoming filled with the true being of Humanity, he is only led into illusions. But he is unaware that they are so; he thinks they have real power to sustain Humanity.

136. Thus, in the time that went before his working upon Earth, Michael had to witness with anxiety and suffering the evolution of mankind. For in this time men eschewed any real contemplation of the Spirit, and thus they severed all the links that connected them with Michael.

A CHRISTMAS STUDY: THE MYSTERY OF THE LOGOS

Our study of the Michael Mystery was irradiated by thoughts of the Mystery of Golgotha. For, in effect, Michael is the Power who leads man towards the Christ along the true way of man's salvation.

But the Michael Mission is one of those that are repeated again and again in rhythmical succession in the cosmic evolution of mankind. In its beneficial influence on earthly mankind it was repeated before the Mystery of Golgotha. It was connected in that time with all the active revelations which the Christ-Force—as yet external to the Earth—had to pour down to the Earth for the unfolding of mankind. After the Mystery of Golgotha, the Michael Mission enters the service of what must now be achieved in earthly humanity through Christ Himself. In its repetitions, the Michael Mission now appears in a changed and ever-progressing form. The point is that it appears in repetitions.

The Mystery of Golgotha, on the other hand, is an all-embracing World-event, taking place once only in the whole course of the cosmic evolution of mankind.

It was only when humanity had reached the unfolding of the Intellectual or Mind-Soul that the ever-continued danger which was there potentially from the beginning—the danger lest humanity's existence should become severed from the existence of the Divine-Spiritual—made itself fully felt.

And in the same manner in which the soul of man loses the conscious experience in and with the Divine-Spiritual Beings, there emerges around him that which we to-day call 'Nature.'

Man no longer sees the essence and being of Humanity in the Divine-Spiritual Cosmos; he sees the accomplished work of the Divine-Spiritual in this earthly realm. To begin with, however, he sees it not in the abstract form in which it is seen to-day—not as physically sensible events and entities held together by those abstract ideal contents which we call

'Natural Laws.' To begin with, he sees it still as Divine-Spiritual Being—Divine-Spiritual Being surging up and down in all that he perceives around him, in the birth and decay of living animals, in the springing and sprouting of the plant-world, in the activity of water-wells and rivers, in cloud and wind and weather. All these processes of being around him represent to him the gestures, deeds and speech of the Divine Being at the foundation of 'Nature.'

Once upon a time, man had seen in the constellations and movements of the stars the deeds and gestures of the Divine Beings of the Cosmos, whose words he was thus able to read in the heavens. In like manner, the 'facts of Nature' now became for him an expression of the Goddess of the Earth. For the Divinity at work in Nature was conceived as feminine.

Far down into the Middle Ages, the relics of this mode of conception were still at work in the souls of men, filling the Intellectual or Mind-Soul with an Imaginative content.

When men of knowledge wanted to bring the 'processes of Nature' to the understanding of their pupils, they spoke of the deeds of the 'Goddess.' It was only with the gradual dawn of the Spiritual Soul that this living study of Nature, filled as it was with inner soul, grew unintelligible to mankind.

The way in which men looked in this direction in the age of the Intellectual or Mind-Soul is reminiscent of the Myth of Persephone and of the mystery that underlies it.

Persephone, the daughter of Demeter, is compelled by the God of the Underworld to follow him into his kingdom. Eventually it is achieved that she spends one-half of the year only in the Nether world and dwells for the remainder of the year in the Upper world.

This Myth of Persephone was still a great and wonderful expression of the way in which Man, in an age of immemorial antiquity, had perceived and known the evolutionary process of the Earth in dream-like clairvoyance.

In primeval times all the world-creative activity had proceeded from the surroundings of the Earth. The Earth itself was only in process of becoming, and moulded its existence in cosmic evolution from out of the activities of the surrounding world. The Divine-Spiritual Beings of the Cosmos were the creators and moulders of the Earth's existence. But when the Earth was far enough advanced to become an independent heavenly body, Divine-Spiritual Being descended from the great Cosmos to the Earth and became the Earth-Divinity. This cosmic fact the dream-like clairvoyance of primeval mankind had seen and known; and of such knowledge the Myth of Persephone remained—but not only this. For indeed, far down even into the Middle Ages, the way in which men sought to know and penetrate into 'Nature' was still a relic of the same ancient knowledge. It was not yet as in these later times, when men only see according to their sense-impressions, i.e., according to that which appears on the surface of the Earth. They still saw according to the forces that work upwards to the surface from the depths of the Earth. And these 'forces of the depths'—the 'forces of the Nether world'—they saw in mutual interplay with the influences of the stars and elements working from the Earth's environment.

The plants in their varied forms grow forth, revealing themselves in many-coloured glory. Therein are at work the forces of Sun and Moon and Stars, together with the forces of the Earth's depths. The ground and foundation for this is given in the minerals, whose existence is entirely conditioned by that part of the cosmic Beings which has become earthly. Through those heavenly forces alone, which have become earthly, rock and stone shoot forth out of the Nether world. The animal kingdom, on the other hand, has not assumed the forces of the earthly depths. It comes into being through those world-forces alone which are at work from the surroundings of the Earth. It owes its growth, development and surging life, its powers of nutrition, its possibilities of movement, to the Sun-forces streaming down to the Earth. And under the influence of the Moon-forces streaming down to the Earth it has the power to reproduce itself. It appears in manifold forms and species because the starry constellations are working in manifold ways from the Cosmos, shaping and moulding this animal life. The animals are, as it were, only placed down here on Earth from out the Cosmos. It is only with their dim life of consciousness that they partake in the earthly realm; with their origin, development and growth, with all that they are in order to be able to perceive and move about, they are no earthly creatures.

This mightily conceived idea of the evolution of the Earth lived once upon a time in mankind. The greatness of the conception is scarcely recognisable any longer in the relics of it which came down to the Middle Ages. To attain this knowledge one must go back, with the true vision of the seer, into very ancient times. For even the physical documents that are extant do not reveal what was really present there in the souls of men, save to those who are able to penetrate to it by a spiritual path.

Now man is not in a position to hold himself so much aloof from the Earth as do the animals. In saying this, we are approaching the Mystery of Humanity as well as the Mystery of the Animal Kingdom. These Mysteries were reflected in the animal cults of the ancient peoples, and above all in that of the Egyptians. They saw the animals as beings who are but guests upon the Earth, and in whom one may perceive the nature and activity of the spiritual world immediately adjoining this earthly realm. And when in pictures they portrayed the human figure in connection with the animal, they were representing to themselves the forms of those elementary, intermediate beings who, though they are indeed in cosmic evolution on the way to humanity, yet purposely refrain from entering the earthly realm, in order not to become human. For there are such elementary, intermediate beings—and in picturing them the Egyptians were but reproducing what they saw. Such beings, however, have not the full self-consciousness of man, to attain to which man had to enter this earthly world so completely as to receive something of this earthly nature into his very own.

Man had to be exposed to the fact that in this earthly world, though the work of the Divine-Spiritual Beings with whom he is connected is indeed present here, yet *it is only their accomplished work.* And just because only the accomplished work, severed from its Divine origin, is present here, therefore the Luciferic and Ahrimanic beings have access to it. Thus it becomes necessary for man to make this realm of the Divine-accomplished work, permeated as it is by Lucifer and Ahriman, the field of action for one part—namely, the earthly part—of his life's development.

So long as man had not progressed to the unfolding of his Intellectual or Mind-Soul, this was possible, without man's nature becoming permanently severed from its original Divine-Spiritual foundation. But when this point was reached, a corruption took place in man—a corruption of the physical, the etheric and the astral bodies. To an ancient science, this corruption was known as something that was living in man's nature. It was known as a thing that was necessary in order that consciousness might advance to self-consciousness in man. In the stream of knowledge that was cultivated in the centres of learning founded by Alexander the Great, there lived an Aristotelianism which, rightly understood, contained this 'corruption' as an essential element in its psychology. It was only in a later time that these ideas were no longer penetrated in their inward essence.

In the ages before the evolution of his Intellectual or Mind-Soul, man was, however, interwoven still with the forces of his Divine-Spiritual origin, so much so that from their cosmic field of action these forces were able to balance and hold in check the Luciferic and Ahrimanic Powers that reach out to man on Earth. And from the human side enough was done by way of co-operation to maintain the balance, in those actions of Ritual and of the Mysteries, wherein the *picture* was unfolded of the Divine-Spiritual Being diving down into the realm of Lucifer and Ahriman and coming forth again triumphant. Hence in times prior to the Mystery of Golgotha we find in the religious rites of different peoples pictorial representations of that which afterwards, in the Mystery of Golgotha, became reality.

When the Intellectual or Mind-Soul was unfolded, it was through the reality alone that man could continue to be preserved from being severed from the Divine-Spiritual Beings who belonged to him. The Divine had to enter inwardly as Being, even *in* the earthly life, into the organisation of the Intellectual or Mind-Soul which, during earthly existence, has its life from what is earthly. This took place through the Divine-Spiritual Logos, Christ, uniting His cosmic destiny with the Earth for the sake of mankind.

Persephone came down to the Earth in order to save the plant kingdom from being obliged to form itself from what belongs only to Earth. That is the descent of a Divine-Spiritual Being into the Nature of the Earth. Persephone, too, has a kind of 'resurrection,' but this takes place annually, in rhythmical succession.

Over against this event—which is also a cosmic event occurring on the Earth—we have for *Humanity* the descent of the Logos. Persephone descends to bring *Nature* into its original direction. In this case there must be rhythm at the foundation; for the events in Nature take place rhythmically. The Logos descends into humanity. This occurs *once* during human evolution. For the evolution of humanity is but *one* part in a gigantic cosmic rhythm, in which, before the stage of man's existence, humanity was something altogether different, and in which, after this stage is passed, it will be something altogether different again; whereas the plant life repeats itself *as such* in shorter rhythms.

From the age of the Spiritual Soul onwards it is necessary for humanity to see the Mystery of Golgotha in this light. For already in the age of the Intellectual or Mind-Soul there would have been a danger of man being separated, if the

Mystery of Golgotha had not taken place. In the age of the Spiritual Soul a complete darkening of the Spirit-world would needs come about for human consciousness, if the Spiritual Soul could not strengthen itself sufficiently to look back in inward vision to its Divine-Spiritual origin. If, however, it is able to do this, it finds the cosmic Logos, as the Being Who can lead it back. It fills itself with the mighty picture which reveals what took place on Golgotha.

The beginning of this understanding is the loving comprehension of the cosmic Christmas, the cosmic Initiation-Night, the festive remembrance of which is celebrated each year. For the Spiritual Soul, which first receives the element of Intellectuality, is strengthened by allowing true love to enter into this, the coldest element of soul. And the warmth of true love is there in its highest form when it goes out to the Jesus child who appears on Earth during the cosmic Initiation-Night. In this way man has allowed the highest earthly Spirit-fact, which was at the same time a physical event, to work upon his soul; he has entered upon the path by which he receives Christ into himself.

Nature must be recognised in such a way that in Persephone—or the Being who was still seen in the early Middle Ages when they spoke of 'Nature'—it reveals the Divine-Spiritual, original and eternal Force out of which it originated and continually originates, as the foundation of earthly human existence.

The world of Man must be so recognised that in Christ it reveals the original and eternal Logos who works for the unfolding of the Spirit-being of man in the sphere of the Divine-Spiritual Being bound up with man from the Beginning.

To turn the human heart in love to these great cosmic facts: this is the true content of the festival of remembrance which approaches man each year when he contemplates the cosmic Initiation-Night of Christmas. If love such as this lives in human hearts, it permeates the cold light-element of the Spiritual Soul with warmth. Were the Spiritual Soul obliged to remain without such permeation, man would never become filled with the Spirit. He would die in the cold of the intellectual consciousness; or he would have to remain in a mental life that did not progress to the unfolding of the conscious Spiritual Soul. He would then come to a stop with the unfolding of the Intellectual or Mind-Soul.

But in its essential nature the Spiritual Soul is not cold. It seems to be so only at the commencement of its unfolding, because at that stage it can only reveal the light-element in its nature, and not as yet the cosmic warmth in which it has indeed its origin.

To feel and experience Christmas in this way will enable the soul to realise *how the glory of the Divine-Spiritual Beings, whose images are revealed in the Stars, announces itself to man, and how man's liberation takes place, within the precincts of the Earth, from the Powers which wish to alienate him from his origin.*

(Christmas, 1924)

Further Leading Thoughts issued from the Goetheanum for the Anthroposophical Society (in connection with the foregoing Christmas Study)

137. The activity in the evolution of the World and Mankind which comes about through the forces of Michael, repeats itself rhythmically, though in ever-changing and progressing forms, before the Mystery of Golgotha and after.

138. The Mystery of Golgotha is the greatest event, occurring once and for all in the evolution of mankind. Here there can be no question of a rhythmic repetition. For while the evolution of mankind also stands within a mighty cosmic rhythm, still it is *one*—one vast member in a cosmic rhythm. Before it became this One, mankind was something altogether different from mankind; afterwards it will again be altogether different. Thus there are many Michael events in

the evolution of mankind, but there is only one event of Golgotha.

139. In the quick rhythmic repetition of the seasons of the year, the Divine-Spiritual Being which descended into the depths of Earth to permeate Nature's process with the Spirit, accomplishes this process. It is the ensouling of Nature with the *Forces* of the Beginning and of Eternity which must remain at work; even as Christ's descent is the ensouling of Mankind with the *Logos* of the Beginning and of Eternity, whose working for the salvation of mankind shall never cease.

HEAVENLY HISTORY—MYTHOLOGICAL HISTORY—EARTHLY HISTORY. THE MYSTERY OF GOLGOTHA

In the spatial Cosmos we have the contrast of the Universal spaces and the Earthly centre. In the Universal spaces the stars, as it were, are scattered wide, while from the Earthly centre forces are streaming out in all directions into the far-spread Universe.

To man as he stands in the world in the present cosmic epoch, it is only as a great totality that the glory of the stars and the working of the earthly forces can represent the finished work of the Divine-Spiritual Beings with whom he in his inner being is connected.

But there was once a cosmic epoch when the glory of the stars and the forces of the Earth were still a direct spiritual revelation of the Divine-Spiritual Beings. At that time, man in his dim consciousness felt the Divine-Spiritual Beings actively working in his own nature.

Another epoch of time ensued. The starry heavens became severed, as a corporeal existence, from the Divine-Spiritual working. There originated what we may call the 'World-spirit' and the 'World-body.' The World-spirit is a multitude of Divine-Spiritual Beings. In the former epoch these Beings had worked from the starry places inward to the Earth. All that had shone forth from universal space, all that had radiated by way of forces from the earthly centre, was in reality Intelligence and Will of the Divine-Spiritual Beings, who were working creatively upon the Earth and Earth-humanity.

In the later cosmic epochs—after the Saturn and Sun-evolutions—the working of the Intelligence and Will of the Divine-Spiritual Beings became more and more spiritually inward. That in which They had been actively present in the beginning became the 'World-body': the harmonious arrangement of stars in universal space. Looking back on these matters with a spiritual world-conception, we may express it thus: From the original spirit-body of the World-creative Beings, the World-spirit and the World-body were evolved. And in the ordering and movement of the stars, the World-body now shews what the Intelligent and Will-imbued working of the Gods *once upon a time* was like. For the cosmic present however, what was once the Divine Intelligence and Will living and moving freely in the stars, has become fastened in the fixed Laws of the starry universe.

To-day, therefore, that which shines inward from the starry worlds to man on Earth is no longer an immediate expression of Divine Will and Divine Intelligence, but it is a sign that has come to stand:—a sign of what the Divine Will and Intelligence was, once upon a time, even in the very stars. Potent as it is to call forth wonder in the human soul, we must recognise in the sublime formation of the starry heavens a revelation of the Gods which is of the past; we cannot perceive in it their present revelation.

That, however, which in the shining of the stars is 'of the past,' is 'present' in the Spirit-world. And in this 'present' Spirit-world, man with his own true being dwells.

Studying the formation of the world, we must look back to an *ancient cosmic epoch* when the World-spirit and the World-body still worked as an undivided unity. Then we must envisage the *middle epoch,* in which they unfold as a duality. And at length we must think into the future—into the *third epoch* when the World-spirit will once again take up the World-body into its active working.

For the old epoch, it would have been impossible to 'calculate' the constellations and the courses of the stars; for these were then the expression of the free Intelligence and free Will of Divine-Spiritual Beings. Moreover, in the future they will once again become 'incalculable.'

'Calculation' has a meaning only for the middle cosmic epoch.

And this holds good, not only of the constellations and the movements of the stars, but of the working of the forces which radiate from the earthly centre to the far-spread Universe. That which works 'out of the depths' also becomes 'calculable.'

Everything strives from the older cosmic epoch towards the middle epoch, when the Spatial and Temporal becomes 'calculable,' and the Divine-Spiritual as manifestation of Intelligence and Will must be sought for 'behind' this 'calculable' world.

Only in this middle epoch are the conditions given for man to progress from a dim state of consciousness to one of free and bright self-conscious being, with a free Intelligence and a free Will of his own.

Thus there had to come the time when Copernicus and Kepler could 'calculate' the body of the world. For it was through the cosmic forces with which this moment was connected, that the self-consciousness of man had to take shape. The seed of man's self-consciousness had been laid in an older time; and now the time was come when it was far enough advanced to 'calculate' the far-spread Universe.

On the Earth, 'History' takes place. What we call 'History' would never have come about if the far spaces of the Universe had not evolved into the 'hard and fast' constellations and starry courses. In 'historic evolution' on the Earth we have an image—albeit thoroughly transformed—of what was once upon a time 'heavenly History.' Earlier peoples still had this 'heavenly History' in their consciousness, and were indeed far more aware of it than of the Earthly.

In earthly History there lives the intelligence and will of men—in connection, to begin with, with the cosmic Will and Intelligence of the Gods; then, independent of them.

In heavenly History, on the other hand, there lived the Intelligence and Will of the Divine-Spiritual Beings who are connected with mankind.

When we look back into the spiritual life of nations, we come to an age of far-distant antiquity when there was present in man a consciousness of being and willing in communion with the Divine-Spiritual Beings—so much so that the History of men was heavenly History. The man of that age, when he came to speak of 'origins,' did not relate earthly events but cosmic. And even in relation to his own present time, that which was going on in his earthly environment seemed to him so insignificant beside the cosmic processes that he gave his attention to the latter only, not to the former.

There was an epoch when humanity was conscious of beholding the history of the heavens in mighty and impressive revelations, wherein the Divine-Spiritual Beings themselves stood before the soul of man. They spoke, and man in Dream-Inspiration hearkened to their speech; they revealed their forms, and in Dream-Imagination man saw them.

This heavenly History, which for a long time filled the souls of men, was followed by the mythical History, generally regarded in our time as a poetic creation of the ancients. Mythical History combines heavenly events with earthly. 'Heroes,' for instance,—super-human beings—appear on the scene. They are beings at a higher stage in evolution than the human being. In a given epoch, for example, man had developed the members of human nature only so far as to the Sentient Soul, but the 'Hero' had already evolved what will one day appear in man as Spirit-Self. In the existing conditions of the Earth, the 'Hero' could not incarnate directly, but he could do so indirectly by diving down into the body of a human being, and thus becoming able to work as a man among men. Such beings are to be seen in the 'Initiates' of an earlier time.

To understand the true position of the facts in this world-process, we must not imagine that in the successive epochs mankind 'conceived' of the processes and events in just this way. But that which actually took place, as between the more spiritual, 'incalculable' and the corporeal, 'calculable' world, underwent a change. Long after the world-relationships had actually changed, human consciousness in this or that nation still held fast to a world-conception corresponding to a far earlier reality. To begin with, this was due to the fact that the consciousness of men, which does not keep pace exactly with the cosmic process, really continued to behold the old condition. Afterwards there came a time in which the vision faded, but men still held fast to the old by tradition. Thus in the Middle Ages an in-playing of the heavenly world into the earthly was still conceived out of tradition, but it was no longer seen, for the force of Imaginative picture-seeing was no longer present.

In the earthly realm, the different peoples evolved in such a way as to hold fast to the content of one or other world-conception for varying periods of time. Thus, world-conceptions which by their nature follow one upon the other are found living side by side. Albeit, the variety of world-conceptions is due not to this alone, but also to the fact that the different nations, according to their inner talents, did really see different spiritual things. Thus the Egyptians beheld the world in which beings dwell who have come to a premature standstill on the path of human evolution and have not become earthly Man. The Egyptians too saw man himself, after his earthly life, in the midst of all that he had to do with beings such as these. The Chaldæan peoples, on the other hand, saw more the way in which extra-earthly spiritual Beings, both good and evil, entered into the earthly life to work there.

The ancient 'Heavenly History' properly speaking, which belonged to a very long epoch of time, was followed by the epoch of Mythological History, shorter, but, in comparison to the subsequent period of 'History' in the accepted sense, none the less very long.

It is, as I explained above, only with difficulty that man in his consciousness takes leave of the old conceptions wherein the Gods and men are thought of in living interplay and co-operation. Thus the period of Earthly History in the proper sense has long been present; it has in fact been present since the unfolding of the Intellectual or Mind-soul. Nevertheless for a long time men continued to 'think' in the sense of what had been before. It was only when the first germs of the Spiritual Soul evolved, that they began therewith to pay attention to what is now called 'History in the proper sense.'

And in this Human-Spiritual element, which, loosed from the Divine-Spiritual, becomes 'History,' the free Intelligence and the free Will can be experienced consciously by men.

Thus the World-process in which man is interwoven, runs its course between the fully calculable and the working of the free Intelligence and the free Will. This World-process manifests itself in all conceivable intermediate shades of co-operation between these two.

Man lives his life between birth and death in such a manner that in the 'calculable' the bodily foundation is created for the unfolding of his inner soul-and-spirit nature, which is free and incalculable. He goes through his life between death and new birth in the incalculable, but in such a way that the calculable there unfolds, in thought, 'within' his existence of soul and spirit. Out of this calculable element he thereby becomes the builder of his coming life on Earth.

That which cannot be calculated is manifested forth on Earth in 'History,' but into it the calculable is incorporated, though only to a slight extent.

The Luciferic and Ahrimanic beings oppose themselves to the order which is established between the incalculable and the calculable by the Divine-Spiritual Beings who have been united with man from the very beginning; they oppose the harmonising of the Cosmos by the Divine-Spiritual Beings through 'measure, number and weight.' Lucifer cannot unite anything calculable with the nature that he has given to his being. His ideal is a cosmic and unconditioned activity of Intelligence and Will.

This Luciferic tendency is in keeping with the cosmic order in the realms in which there should be happenings that are free. And Lucifer is there the competent spiritual helper of the unfolding of humanity. Without his assistance freedom could not enter into the human life of spirit and soul which is built on the foundation of the calculable bodily nature. But Lucifer would like to extend this tendency to the whole Cosmos. And in this, his activity becomes a conflict against the Divine-Spiritual order to which man originally belongs.

At this point Michael steps in. With his own being he stands within the incalculable; but he balances the incalculable with the calculable, which he bears within him as the cosmic Thought that he has received from his Gods.

The position of the Ahrimanic Powers in the world is different. They are the exact opposite of the Divine-Spiritual Beings with whom man is originally united. At the present time these latter are purely spiritual Powers who possess absolutely free Intelligence and absolutely free Will, but in this Intelligence and Will they create the wise insight of the necessity of the calculable and the unfree—the cosmic Thought out of whose lap man is to unfold as a free being. And in the Cosmos they are united *in love* with all that is calculable—with the cosmic Thought. This love streams from them through the Universe.

In complete contrast with this, there lives, in the greedy desire of the Ahrimanic powers, *cold hatred* against all that unfolds in freedom. Ahriman's efforts are directed towards making a cosmic machine out of that which he allows to stream forth from the Earth into universal space. His ideal is 'measure, number and weight' and nothing else than these. He was called into the Cosmos that serves the evolution of humanity, because 'measure, number and weight,' which is his sphere, had to be unfolded.

The world is truly understood only by one who comprehends it *everywhere* with respect to spirit and body. This must be carried right into Nature, with respect to such Powers as the Divine-Spiritual who work in love and the Ahrimanic who work in hatred. In Nature's cosmic warmth which comes in spring and works more strongly towards summer, we must perceive the love of the Divine-Spiritual Beings working through Nature; in the icy blast of winter we must become aware of Ahriman's working.

At midsummer, Lucifer's power weaves itself into the love that works in Nature:—into the warmth. At Christmas the power of the Divine-Spiritual Beings with whom man is originally united is directed against the frost-hatred of Ahriman. And towards spring the Divine Love working in Nature continually softens down the Ahriman-hatred there.

The appearance of this Divine Love which comes each year is a time of remembrance, for with Christ the free element of God entered into the calculable element of Earth. Christ works in absolute freedom in the calculable element, and in this way He renders innocuous the Ahrimanic which craves for the calculable alone.

The Event of Golgotha is the free cosmic deed of love within Earthly History, and it can only be grasped by the love which man develops for its comprehension.

(About Christmas, 1924)

Further Leading Thoughts issued from the Goetheanum for the Anthroposophical Society (in connection with the foregoing on the subject of Heavenly History, Mythological History, Earthly History, the Mystery of Golgotha)

140. The cosmic process in which the evolution of mankind is interwoven—reflected, in the consciousness of man, as 'History' in the widest sense—reveals the following successive epochs: a long epoch of 'Heavenly History'; a shorter epoch of 'Mythological History'; and the epoch, relatively very short, of 'Earthly History.'

141. To-day, this cosmic process is divided, into the working of Divine-Spiritual Beings in free Intelligence and Will which none can calculate, and the 'calculable' process of the World-body.

142. Against the calculable order of the World-body the Luciferian Powers stand opposed; against all that creates in free Intelligence and Will, the Ahrimanic.

143. The Event of Golgotha is a cosmic deed, and free. Springing from the Universal love, it is intelligible only by the love in Man.

WHAT IS REVEALED WHEN ONE LOOKS BACK INTO REPEATED LIVES ON EARTH

When we are able to look back with spiritual knowledge into the former Earth-lives of a human being, we find that there are a number of such lives in which man was already a 'person.' His outward form was similar to what it is to-day, and he had an inner life of individual stamp and character. Earthly lives emerge, revealing that the Intellectual or Mind-Soul was present in them, but not as yet the Spiritual Soul; others appear, in which only the Sentient Soul was developed—and so forth.

We find it so in the epochs of Earthly History, and indeed it was so long before these epochs.

But as we look back still farther, we come into ages of time when it was not yet so—ages in which we find Man interwoven still, both in his inner life and in his outer formation, with the world of Divine-Spiritual Beings. Man is already there as earthly man, but he is not yet detached from Divine-Spiritual Being, Thinking and Willing.

And in yet earlier epochs man as a separate being disappears altogether; there are present only the Divine-Spiritual Beings, bearing man within them.

Man has undergone these three stages of evolution during his earthly time. The transition from the first to the second took place in the latest epoch of Lemuria; that from the second to the third in Atlantean times.

Now just as in his present earthly life man bears his experiences within him in the shape of memory, so does he bear within him as a cosmic memory all that he has undergone in the way above described.

What is the earthly life of the soul? It is the world of our memories, ready at every moment to have fresh perceptions. In this interplay of memory and fresh experience, man lives his inner life on Earth.

But this inner life on Earth could not unfold at all if there were not present still in man, as a cosmic memory, what we see when we look back with spiritual vision into the first stage of his becoming Earthly Man—the stage in which he was not yet detached from Divine-Spiritual Being.

Of all that took place in the world at that time, there is livingly present on the Earth to-day, that alone which is unfolded within the human system of nerves and senses. In outer Nature, all the forces that were then at work have died and can now only be seen in their dead forms.

Thus in the human world of Thought there lives as a present manifestation something which, in order to have earthly existence, requires as its basis the very thing that was already evolved in man before he attained individual, earthly being.

Every time he passes through the life between death and a new birth, man experiences this stage anew. But into the world of Divine-Spiritual Beings, which receives him again even as it once entirely contained him—into this world he now carries his full individual existence which has taken shape during his lives on Earth. Between death and a new birth, man is indeed in the present, but he is living also in all the time that he has undergone through repeated lives on Earth and lives between death and a new birth.

It is different with that which lives in the Feeling-world of man. This is related to those experiences of the past which came immediately after the ones in which man was yet unmanifest as such. It is related, that is to say, to experiences which man already underwent as man but when he was not yet separated from Divine-Spiritual Being, Thinking and Willing. Man in the present could not unfold the world of Feeling if it did not arise on the foundation of his rhythmic system. And in his rhythmic system we have the cosmic memory of the above-described second stage of his evolution.

Thus in the world of Feeling the 'present' in the human soul is working together with that which works on in him from an ancient time.

In the life between death and a new birth, man experiences the contents of the epoch of which we are here speaking as the boundary of his Cosmos. What the starry heavens are to man in the physical life on Earth, his existence between his full union with the Divine-Spiritual world and his severance from it, is to him spiritually in the life between death and a new birth. In that life, there appear to him at the 'world-boundary', not the physical heavenly bodies, but in the place of each star the sum-total of Divine-Spiritual Beings, who, as we know, are in reality the star.

Connected with the Will alone and not with Feeling or with Thought, there lives in man that which is manifested by those earthly lives which, when we look back on them, reveal already the personal, individual character. That which from cosmic sources gives to man his outer form, is preserved in this outer form as a cosmic memory. This cosmic memory lives in the human form as a totality of forces. But these are not the immediate forces of the Will; they represent that in the human organism which is the foundation of the forces of the Will.

In the life between death and a new birth, *this* region of the human being lies beyond the 'world-boundary.' Man there conceives of it as of something that will belong to him once more in his new life on Earth.

In his system of nerves and senses, man is to-day still united with the Cosmos in the way he was when he was manifest only germinally within the Divine-Spiritual womb.

In his rhythmic system, man is to-day still living in the Cosmos in the way he lived when he was already there as man, but not yet detached from the Divine-Spiritual.

In his system of metabolism and limbs—the foundation for the unfolding of his Will—man lives in such a way that all that he has undergone in his personal individual lives on Earth, ever since these began, and in his lives between death and a new birth, works on within this system.

From the forces of the Earth, man receives that alone

which gives him consciousness of self. The physical bodily foundation of self-consciousness is due also to what the Earth brings about. But everything else in the human being has a cosmic origin, external to the Earth.

The sentient and thought-bearing astral body with its etheric-physical foundation, all the moving life in the etheric body, and even that which works physico-chemically in the physical body, is of extra-earthly origin. Strange as this may seem, the physico-chemical which is at work within the human being is not derived from the Earth.

The fact that man evolves this extra-earthly, cosmic life within him, is due to the working of the *planets* and other *stars*. All that he thus unfolds, the *Sun* with its forces carries to the Earth. By the Sun, the human-cosmic element is transplanted into the earthly realms. By the Sun, man lives as a heavenly being on the Earth. And that alone, whereby he transcends his own human formation—namely, his power to bring forth his kind—is a gift of the Moon.

Needless to say these are not the only influences of Sun and Moon. Lofty spiritual influences also proceed from them.

When about Christmas-time the Sun increases more and more in power for the Earth, it is the yearly influence—manifesting *rhythmically* in the physical-earthly realm—which is an expression of the Spirit in Nature. The evolution of mankind is a single member in what we may describe as a gigantic cosmic year, as will be evident from our preceding studies. And in this cosmic year the cosmic Christmas is at the point where the Sun not only works towards the Earth out of the Spirit of Nature, but where the Christ-Spirit, the Soul of the Sun, descends on to the Earth.

As in the single human being what he experiences individually is connected with the cosmic memory, so will the human soul have a right feeling of the yearly Christmas when he conceives the heavenly and cosmic Christ-Event as *working on and on*, comprehending it as a memory not only human but cosmic. For at Christmas-time not only man remembers in celebration the descent of Christ, but the Cosmos does so too.

(about New Year, 1925)

Further Leading Thoughts issued from the Goetheanum for the Anthroposophical Society (with respect to the preceding study: 'What is revealed when one looks back into repeated Lives on Earth')

144. Looking back into a human being's repeated lives on Earth, we find three distinct stages. In a remote past, man did not exist with individuality of being, but as a germ in the Divine and Spiritual. As we look back into this stage we find not yet a human being but Divine-Spiritual Beings: the Primal Forces, Principalities or Archai.

145. This was followed by an intermediate stage. Man existed already with individuality of being, but he was not yet detached from the Thinking and Willing and Being of the Divine-Spiritual World. At this stage he had not yet his present personality, with which he appears on Earth as a being completely self-possessed, detached from the Divine-Spiritual World.

146. The present condition is the third and latest. Here man experiences himself in human form and figure, detached from the Divine-Spiritual World; and he experiences the world as an environment with which he stands face to face, individually and personally. This stage began in Atlantean time.

WHAT IS REVEALED WHEN ONE LOOKS BACK INTO FORMER LIVES BETWEEN DEATH AND A NEW BIRTH

A study in two parts: Part one.

In our last study we followed human life as a whole by turning our attention to the successive lives on Earth. The second point of view, which can throw still more light upon what was revealed by the first, is yielded when we consider the successive lives between death and new birth.

Here also we see that the content of these lives, such as they are at the present time, goes back only to a certain point of time in earthly evolution. Their content is determined by the circumstance that man carries with him through the gate of death the inward power of self-consciousness gained in earthly life. This also enables him to confront as an individual the Divine-Spiritual Beings into whose presence he comes.

This was not the case in a preceding period. At that time man had not yet progressed very far in the unfolding of his self-consciousness. The power gained on Earth was insufficient to detach him from the Divine-Spiritual Beings and so give him individual existence between death and new birth. Not that man was then within the Divine-Spiritual Beings, but he was within their sphere of influence, so that his will was essentially *their* will, *not* his own.

Before this period there lies another in which, as we look back, we do not meet with man in his present constitution of soul and spirit at all, but we find a world of Divine-Spiritual Beings within whom man only exists germinally. These Beings are the Primal Forces, the Archai.

And indeed, if we trace back the life of one human being, we find not one Divine-Spiritual Being but all the Beings that belong to this Hierarchy.

In these Divine-Spiritual Beings lives the will that man shall be. The will of all these Beings plays a part in the 'becoming' of each single human being. The cosmic aim of their harmonious co-operation is the production of the human *form*; for man is still without form in the Divine-Spiritual World.

It may seem strange that the whole choir of Divine-Spiritual Beings should work for a single human being. But the Hierarchies of the Exusiai, Dynamis, Kyriotetes, Thrones, Cherubim and Seraphim also worked in this way at a still earlier stage throughout the Moon, Sun and Saturn evolutions, in order that man might come into being.

What had previously originated as a kind of pre-human being on Saturn, Sun and Moon, had no uniform shape. Some of these pre-human beings were chiefly organised with respect to the limbs-system, others with respect to the breast-system, others again with respect to the head-system. These were actual human beings; we describe them here as pre-human only in order to distinguish them from the later stage, when the union of all these systems appears in the human form. The differentiation among them goes even further, for we may speak of heart-men, lung-men, etc.

The Hierarchy of the Primal Forces considered it their task to lead into the general human form all these pre-human beings, whose soul-life also corresponded to their one-sided formation. They took over Man from the hands of the Exusiai. The latter had already *in thought* created unity out of the human multiplicity; but among the Exusiai this unity was still an ideal form, a World-thought-form. Out of this the Archai moulded the etheric form, and this form already contained the forces which made it possible for the physical shape to originate.

When we observe these things a stupendous fact is revealed, viz., that man is the ideal and aim of Gods. But this vision cannot be for man the source of vanity and pride; for he may only reckon, as coming from himself, what he has with full self-consciousness made out of himself during earthly life. And, expressed in cosmic proportions, this is little as compared with that foundation for his individual being which the Gods have created out of the macrocosm which they themselves are, as the microcosm, which he is. The Divine-Spiritual Beings confront one another in the Cosmos. The visible expression of this fact is the form of the starry heavens. They wished to create in a unity as Man all that they themselves are as a choir.

In order really to understand what the whole choir of the Hierarchy of the Archai accomplished when they created the human form, we must remember that there is a very great difference between this form and the physical body of man. The physical body is made up of the physical and chemical processes in man. These processes take place in the present human being within the human form. But this form itself is something that is *altogether spiritual*. It ought to fill us with solemn feelings when, on looking at the human form, we realise that with physical senses we are perceiving in the physical world something that is spiritual. For one who is able to see spiritually it is really the case that in the human form he sees a true Imagination which has descended into the physical world. If we wish to see Imaginations we must pass from the physical world to the neighbouring spiritual world, and then we realise how the human form is related to these Imaginations.

When with the inner vision of the soul man looks back over the lives between death and a new birth he finds a first period during which this human form originated. And at the same time the deeper relation that exists between man and the Hierarchy of the Archai is revealed.

During this period there is just an indication of the difference between earthly life and the life between death and new birth. For the Hierarchy of the Archai works in rhythmical epochs at the development of the human form. In one period of their work the Archai direct the thoughts which guide their several wills more towards the Cosmos beyond the Earth; at another time they look down to the Earth. And out of the co-operation of what is aroused from the Cosmos and from the Earth the human form is developed, which is thus the expression of the fact that man is an Earth-being and at the same time an extra-earthly, cosmic being.

But the human form, here described as the creation of the Hierarchy of the Archai, comprises not merely the external outline of man and the formation of the surface as it is determined by the limit of the skin, but also the formation of the forces contained in his carriage, in his power of movement, which is adapted to the conditions on the Earth, and in the capacity to use his body as a means whereby to express his inner being.

It is owing to this creative work of the Hierarchy of the Archai that man is able to assume his upright position within the earthly conditions of gravity, that within these conditions he can maintain his balance while moving freely, that he can liberate his arms and hands from the force of gravity and use them freely—all this he owes to the Archai, in addition to much more that lies within him and yet has form. All this is prepared during the life which may also for this period be called the life between death and a new birth. It is here prepared in such a manner that, in the third period, at the present time, man is himself able, during his life between death and a new birth, to work at this form for his earthly existence.

(New Year, 1925)

Further Leading Thoughts issued from the Goetheanum for the Anthroposophical Society (in connection with the foregoing study: What is revealed when one looks back into former lives between death and a new birth?)

147. Man's lives between death and a new birth also show three distinct periods. In the first of these, he lived entirely within the Hierarchy of the Archai, who prepared, for the

physical world, the human form and figure which he was afterwards to bear.

148. Thus the Archai prepared the human being subsequently to unfold the free Self-consciousness. For this Self-consciousness can only evolve in beings who can show it forth, in the form and figure which was here created, out of an inner impulse of the soul.

149. In this we see how qualities and powers of Mankind, becoming manifest in the present cosmic age, were laid down in germ in ages long gone by. We see how the Microcosm grows out of the Macrocosm.

WHAT IS REVEALED WHEN ONE LOOKS BACK INTO FORMER LIVES BETWEEN DEATH AND A NEW BIRTH

Part Two

In a second period man passes from the realm of the Archai to that of the Archangeloi. With these, however, he is no longer united in so bodily-spiritual a way as he was with the Archai. His union with the Hierarchy of the Archangeloi is more purely spiritual. But it is still so intimate that he cannot yet be said to have been severed in this period from the Divine-Spiritual world.

The Archangeloi Hierarchy gives to man for his etheric body that which corresponds in it to the form in the physical, which he owes to the Archai. The physical body, through its form, is adapted to the Earth in such a way as to become on Earth the vehicle of self-consciousness. In like manner the etheric body is adapted to the extra-earthly cosmic forces and relationships of forces. In the physical body lives the Earth; in the etheric the world of the stars. All the inner forces which man bears within him in such a way that while he is on Earth he does at the same time, in his posture, movement and gesture, emancipate himself from the Earth, he owes to the creation of the Archangeloi in his etheric body. As the Earth-forces are able to live in the physical body through its formation, so in the etheric body there live the forces which stream down on all sides from the encircling Cosmos to the Earth. The Earth-forces living in the physically visible formation of the body are those which make the form of man relatively complete, hard and fast within itself. Subject to a certain metamorphosis, the main outlines of man remain hard and fast throughout his earthly life. His faculties of movement, too, have hardened into permanent habits and the like. In the etheric body on the other hand, there is perpetual mobility, mirroring the constellations of the stars as they change during the earthly life of man. The etheric body shapes itself even in accordance with the changes in the heavens as between day and night; and it does so also with the changes that take place between the birth and death of the man concerned.

This adaptation of the etheric body to the heavenly forces is not in contradiction to the gradual severance of the starry heavens from the Divine-Spiritual Powers, mentioned in earlier studies. It is true to say that in very ancient times Divine Will and Divine Intelligence were living in the stars, and that in later times the stars passed over into the "calculable". Through what has now become their finished work, the Gods are no longer working upon man. Nevertheless, through his etheric body man gradually achieves a relationship of his own to the stars, just as he does through his physical body to earthly gravity.

What man incorporates into his nature when at birth he descends from the Spirit-world on the Earth—namely the etheric body which absorbs the extra-earthly, cosmic forces—is created in this second period by the Hierarchy of the Archangeloi.

One of the essential features which man receives through this Hierarchy is his membership of a group of human beings on the Earth. Humanity is differentiated over the face of the Earth. Looking back into this second period, it is not, however, the present differentiation of races and nations that we find, but a somewhat different—a more spiritual one. It is due to the fact that the starry forces strike the different places of the Earth in varying constellations. For on the Earth itself—in the distribution of land and water, in climate, vegetation and the like—the starry heavens are indeed active. Inasmuch as man must adapt himself to *these* conditions, which are really there as heavenly conditions on the Earth, such adaptation belongs to his etheric body; and the forming of the latter is a creative work of the choir of Archangeloi.

But now it is just in this second period that the Luciferic

and Ahrimanic Powers enter the life of man in a peculiar degree. Their entry is necessary, albeit to begin with it may seem to be driving man *beneath* the level of his true nature.

If man is to develop self-consciousness in his earthly life, he must get loose from the Divine-Spiritual world from which he originally proceeded, in greater measure than that world itself can bring about. This is what takes place in the time when the Archangeloi are at work upon him. For his union with the Spirit-world is no longer as firm as it was when the Archai were at work upon him. Lucifer and Ahriman are more able to grapple with the spiritual forces proceeding from the Archangeloi, than with the stronger forces of the Archai.

The Luciferic Powers permeate the etheric formation of man with a more intense inclination towards the starry world than it would have if the Divine-Spiritual Powers, originally united with man, were alone at work. The Ahrimanic Powers entwine his physical formation more tightly in the realm of earthly gravity than would have been the case if they were unable to exert their influence.

By this means the seed of full self-consciousness and of free will is planted into man. Much as the Ahrimanic Powers hate free will, *in man*—by tearing him loose from *his* Divine-Spiritual world—they bring about the germinal beginnings of free will.

To begin with, however, during the second period itself, that which the various Hierarchies from the Seraphim down to the Archangeloi have brought about in man, is impressed into his physical and etheric bodies more deeply than would have been possible without the Luciferic and Ahrimanic influence. For without this influence, the working of the Hierarchies would remain more in the astral body and the Ego.

Thus it happened that the more spiritual grouping of mankind over the face of the Earth, which the Archangeloi were striving for, did not take place.

Being pressed down into the physical and etheric body, the

spiritual forces are transformed into their opposite. In place of something more spiritual, the differentiation of races and nations comes about.

Without the Luciferic and Ahrimanic influence, human beings on Earth would see themselves differentiated by forces working downwards from the heavens. The different groups would be to one another in their life like beings who willingly with love, give to one another of the spiritual and receive in turn. In races and nations it is earthly gravity which appears through the human body; in the spiritual groupings a mirrored image of the Divine-Spiritual world would have appeared.

With all this, the beginnings of what afterwards became the full self-consciousness of man had to be implanted in his evolution already at that time. And this meant that—in a mitigated form, it is true, but yet in a certain way—the primeval differentiation of humanity which existed when man passed over from the Hierarchy of the Exusiai to that of the Archai remained preserved.

Man—as it were in a cosmic school—experienced this stage in his evolution, contemplating it with inner feeling. True, he did not yet develop a knowledge of the fact that this was an essential preparation for his subsequent self-consciousness. But his feeling vision of the forces of his evolution at that time was none the less important for the incorporation of self-consciousness into his astral body and his Ego.

With respect to Thought, the following took place. By the Luciferic Powers man was informed with the tendency still to immerse himself in the old forms of the Spiritual, instead of adapting himself to the new. Lucifer indeed always has this striving to conserve for man the earlier forms of his life.

By this means human Thinking was evolved. In the life between death and a new birth man gradually developed that faculty which in primeval times had formed the thoughts in him. It was a faculty which *at that time* could behold the

Spiritual, though it was like what is now mere sense-perception. For at that time the Physical still carried the Spiritual upon its surface. To-day, however, the faculty of thought preserved from that time can only work as restricted sense-perception. Man's power to lift himself in thought to the spiritual world gradually declined. This became fully evident at length when in the age of the Spiritual Soul the spiritual world was veiled for man in complete darkness. Thus in the nineteenth century it came about that the best men of science, unable to become materialists, declared: We have no alternative but to limit our research to that world which can be investigated by measure, number and weight and by the senses. We have, however, no right to deny a spiritual world, hidden beneath this world of Nature. In such words they indicated that there might be a world full of light, *unknown to man*, where man can only stare into an empty darkness.

And as Thought in man was misdirected by Lucifer, so was Will by Ahriman. Man's will was endowed with a tendency to a kind of freedom which he should have entered only at a later stage. This freedom is not real; it is but the illusion of freedom. Men lived in this illusion of freedom for a long time, and thereby became unable to evolve the idea of freedom in a truly spiritual way. They vacillated to and fro, between the one opinion and the other: that man is free, or that he is involved in a sphere of rigid necessity. And when with the spiritual Age of Consciousness true freedom came, they were unable to recognise it, because their powers of perception had too long become entangled in the illusion of freedom.

All that had sunk into the being of man during this second stage in the evolution of his lives between death and a new birth, he carried as a cosmic memory into the third, in which he still lives to-day. In this third stage he is related to the Hierarchy of the Angeloi as in the second to that of the Archangeloi. Only, this relationship to the Angeloi is such that through it the full independent individuality comes into being. For the Angeloi—not the chorus this time, but one Angelos for one human being—restrict themselves to the task of bringing about the right relation of the life between death and a new birth and the life on Earth.

A fact that may seem remarkable to begin with is this. For the *individual* human being in the second stage in the evolution of his lives between death and a new birth the whole Hierarchy of Archangeloi was working. Afterwards the guidance of nations and tribes becomes the task of this Hierarchy, and there is then one Archangelos as the Folk-Spirit for one nation. In the races the Primal Forces or Archai remain at work. Here again, for one race, one Being of the Hierarchy of the Primal Forces works as the Race-Spirit.

Thus the man of present time contains, in the life between death and a new birth also, the cosmic memory of earlier stages of his life. And in the physical world too, where something of spiritual guidance appears as it does in the races and nations, this cosmic memory is most distinctly present.

(New Year, 1925)

Further Leading Thoughts issued from the Goetheanum for the Anthroposophical Society (with respect to the foregoing study [part two]: What is revealed when one looks back into former Lives between Death and a new Birth?)

150. In a second period of evolution of the lives between death and a new birth, man entered the domain of the Archangeloi. The seed of his later conscious Selfhood— prepared for, in the first period, in the forming of the human figure—was now implanted in the nature of his soul.

151. During this second period he was driven by Luciferic

and Ahrimanic influences more deeply into the physical than would have happened without their intervention.

152. In the third period, man enters the domain of the Angeloi, who only wield their influence, however, in the astral body and the Ego. This third period is the present; but what took place in the two former ones still lives on in human evolution and explains the fact that in the nineteenth century—within the age of the Spiritual Soul—man stared into the spiritual world as into vacant darkness.

WHAT IS THE EARTH IN REALITY WITHIN THE MACROCOSM?

In these studies we have contemplated the evolution of the Cosmos and Humanity from the most varied points of view. We have seen how man derives from the extra-earthly Cosmos the forces of his being, with the exception of those that give him self-consciousness. These come to him from the Earth.

The significance of the earthly realm for man is thus explained. But in this connection the question must arise: What is the significance of the earthly realm for the macrocosm?

In order to approach the answer to this question, we must turn our attention once more to what has already been described in these pages.

The consciousness of the seer finds the macrocosm increasingly alive, the more his vision penetrates into the past. In the far distant past, the macrocosm so lives that there ceases to be any question of 'calculating' the manifestations of its life. Out of this living condition man is then brought forth as a separate being, while the macrocosm enters more and more into the 'calculable' sphere.

But in this it undergoes a slow process of death. In the same measure in which man—the microcosm—arises as an independent being from the macrocosm, the macrocosm dies.

In the present cosmic time, a dead macrocosm is existing. But it was not only man who arose in the process of its evolution. The Earth too came forth out of the macrocosm.

Deriving from the Earth the forces for his self-consciousness, man is far too close to it in his inner life to perceive its nature clearly. In the age of the Spiritual Soul, with the full unfolding of self-consciousness, we have grown accustomed to focus our attention on the *spatial* magnitude of the Universe, and to look on the Earth as a speck of dust, insignificant compared to the great universe of physical space.

Hence it will seem strange, to begin with, when spiritual

vision unfolds the true cosmic significance of this alleged 'particle of dust.'

In the mineral ground of the Earth the other kingdoms of Nature—the animal and plant kingdoms—are imbedded. In all this there live the forces which manifest themselves in varied forms of appearance through the seasons. Consider the world of plants. In autumn and winter it manifests the physically dying forces. In this form of appearance, the consciousness of the seer perceives the nature of those forces which have brought about the gradual death of the macrocosm. In spring and summer, forces of growth, springing and sprouting forces, show themselves in the plant life. In the growing, sprouting process, the seer's consciousness perceives not only what brings forth the abundant blessing of the plant life for the given year, but an *excess*. It is an excess of *germinating force*. The plants contain more germinating force than they expend upon the growth of foliage, flower and fruit. For the consciousness of the seer, this excess of germinating force flows out into the extra-earthly macrocosm.

Now in the same manner a surplus of force streams out from the mineral kingdom to the extra-earthly Cosmos. *This* force has the task of carrying the forces from the plant-world to the right places in the macrocosm. Under the influence of the mineral forces, the plant-forces become a newly fashioned picture of a macrocosm.

Likewise there are forces proceeding from the animal nature. These however do not work, like the plant and mineral forces, radiating from the Earth. They work in such a way that the plant-nature, which the mineral forces carry in clear formation into the great Universe, is gathered into a sphere, so that the picture arises of a macrocosm compact and self-contained on all sides.

It is thus the spirit-seeing consciousness beholds the essence of the earthly realm, *which stands as a new, life-kindling element within the dead and dying macrocosm.*

As when the old plant has died and fallen away, the new

plant, however large, is formed again from the seed in space so insignificant and small—so while the old dead macrocosm falls asunder a new macrocosm is coming forth from this 'speck of dust,' the Earth.

It is a true contemplation of the Earth-nature which sees in it on all hands a germinating universe. We only learn to understand the kingdoms of Nature around us when we feel in them the presence of this germinating life.

In the midst of it man fulfils his Earth-existence. He partakes in the germinating life as well as in the dead and dying. From the dead he derives the forces of his thought. In the past, when the forces of his thought were coming forth from the still living macrocosm, they did not provide the foundation for self-conscious humanity. They lived, as growth-forces, in a human being who did not yet possess self-consciousness. *For themselves*, the forces of thought must not have life of their own if they are to provide a basis for the free self-consciousness of man. With the macrocosm whose life has gone out, they for themselves must be the dead *shadows* of what once was living in the primeval Cosmos.

On the other side man shares in the germinating life of the Earth, from which he has the forces of his will. These forces are indeed life itself, but with his self-consciousness man does not take part in their real nature. Deep down within the human being they radiate into the shadows of his thought. The shadows of thought flow through them, and in the flowing of free thought as it unfolds within the germinating earthly nature, the full and free human self-consciousness enters into man during this age of the Spiritual Soul.

The past throwing its shadows, the future fraught with the germs of a new reality meet in the human being; and their meeting constitutes the human life of present time.

That these things are so, is clearly revealed to the consciousness of the seer the moment he enters that spirit-region which immediately adjoins the physical and in which the active presence of Michael is found.

The life of all this earthly realm becomes clear and transparent when we feel at its foundation the germ of a new Universe. Every single plant and stone appears in a new light to the soul of man when he becomes aware that each of these creations is contributing by its life or by its form to this great fact: that the Earth in its unity is an embryo—the seed of a macrocosm newly rising into life.

One should but try to make the thought of these things fully living in oneself, and one will feel how much it may signify for the human heart and mind.

(January, 1925)

Further Leading Thoughts issued from the Goetheanum for the Anthroposophical Society (in connection with the foregoing study: What is the Earth in reality within the Macrocosm?)

153. In the beginning of the age of the Spiritual Soul, it became the custom to turn attention to the physically spatial greatness of the Universe. Impressed above all by this immensity of physical appearance, men speak of the Earth as a mere speck of dust within the Universe.

154. To the consciousness of the seer this 'speck of dust,' the Earth, is revealed as the germ and beginning of a new-rising Macrocosm, while the old Macrocosm appears as a thing whose life has died away. For the old Macrocosm had to die, that man might sever himself from it with full Self-consciousness.

155. In the cosmic present, man partakes: with the Thought-forces that make him free, in the dead Macrocosm; and with the Will-forces, whose essence is concealed from him, in the germinating of this Earth-existence—the Macrocosm newly springing into life.

SLEEPING AND WAKING
IN THE LIGHT OF RECENT STUDIES

In the study of Anthroposophy, sleeping and waking have been dealt with often and from varied points of view. But our understanding of these facts of life must be deepened and refreshed again and again, when other points in the constitution of the world have been considered by us. Our previous explanation, showing how the Earth is the seed of a newly-arising macrocosm, will give us fresh possibilities for a deeper understanding of sleeping and waking.

In the waking state, man lives in the Thought-shadows cast by a dead and dying world, and in the Will-impulses into the inner nature of which, with his ordinary consciousness, he can no more penetrate than into the processes of deep, dreamless sleep.

Where sub-conscious impulses of Will flow into the shadows of Thought, the free dominion of self-consciousness arises. In this self-consciousness, the human 'Ego' lives.

While man experiences his environment in this condition, his inner feeling is permeated by extra-earthly, cosmic impulses, entering from a remote and cosmic past into the present time. He does not become conscious of this fact. For a being can only become conscious of things in which it partakes with its own, dying forces, and not with the growing forces that are the creative kindlers of its life. Thus man experiences himself in consciousness while that which lies at the basis of his inner being is lost to the eye of his mind. And by this very fact he is able, during the waking state, to feel himself so entirely within his shadowed Thoughts. There is no glimmer of life to hinder the full absorption of his inner being in the dead and dying. But from this his 'life in the dead and dying,' the essential being of the earthly sphere conceals the fact that it is in reality the seed of a new Universe. Man in the waking state does not perceive the Earth in its true nature. The cosmic life that is germinating in the Earth escapes him.

Thus man lives in what the Earth gives to him as the basis of his self-consciousness. In the age of unfolding of the self-conscious Ego, the true form both of his inner impulses and of his outer environment is lost to his mind's eye. But as he thus hovers over the true being of the world, he experiences in consciousness the being of the 'I': he experiences himself as a self-conscious being. Above him is the extra-earthly Cosmos; beneath him, in the earthly realm, a world whose true essence is hidden from him. But in between, the free 'I' manifests itself, its essence radiating out in the full light of knowledge and of free volition.

It is different in the sleeping state. In sleep, man lives in his astral body and Ego in the germinating life of the Earth. The strongest 'urge into new life' is there in the environment of man in dreamless sleep. His dreams too are permeated by this life, though not so intensely as to prevent him from experiencing them in a kind of semi-consciousness. Gazing half-consciously upon his dreams, man witnesses the creative forces whereby he himself is woven out of the Cosmos. Even while the dream lights up, the Astral—kindling man to life—becomes visible as it flows into the etheric body. In this lighting-up of dreams, Thought is *still alive.* It is only after man wakens that Thought is gathered up into the forces whereby it dies and becomes a shadow.

This connection between our dream-conceptions and our waking thoughts is of the greatest significance. Man *thinks* within the sphere of those very forces whereby he grows and lives. Yet he cannot become a thinker until these forces die.

At this point there dawns in us a true understanding of why it is that man takes hold of the reality of things in Thought. For in his thoughts he possesses the dead picture of that which, working from the fully living reality of the world, builds and creates him.

It is the dead picture. But this dead picture proceeds from the work of the greatest painter—from the very Cosmos. It is true that the life remains out of it. If it did not, the Ego of man could not unfold. Nevertheless, the full content of the Universe, in all its greatness, is contained within this picture.

So far as was possible at that time and in that context, I indicated this inner relation of Thought and World-reality in my 'Philosophy of Freedom.' It is in the passage of that book where I say that there is indeed a bridge leading from the thinking Ego's depths to the depths of Nature's reality.

Sleep extinguishes the ordinary consciousness because it carries us into the germinating life of Earth—the Earth as it springs forth into the new, living Macrocosm. When the extinction is overcome by Imaginative consciousness, there stands before the human soul—not a sharply outlined Earth in mineral, plant and animal kingdoms of Nature—but a vital process, kindled to life within this Earth and flaming forth into the Macrocosm.

It is thus: In the waking state man must lift himself with his own Ego-being out of the being of the world, in order to attain to free self-consciousness. And in sleep he unites with the being of the world once more.

Such is the rhythm in the present moment of cosmic time: the rhythm of man's earthly existence outside the inner being of the world while he experiences his own being in consciousness, and of his existence within the inner being of the world where the consciousness of his own being is extinguished.

In the condition between death and a new birth, the human Ego lives within the Beings of the Spirit-world. Then, everything that was withdrawn from man's consciousness during his waking life on Earth comes into it again. The macrocosmic forces emerge from their full state of life in a far distant past to their dead and dying nature in the present. And there emerge the earthly forces—the seed of the new-living macrocosm. Then the human being looks into his sleeping states as clearly as in his earthly life he looks forth upon the Earth that glistens in the sunlight.

The Macrocosm, as it is to-day, has indeed become a thing of death. Yet it is through this alone that between death and a new birth man can undergo a life which signifies, compared to the waking life on Earth, a loftier awakening. For it is indeed an awakening, whereby he becomes able fully to control the forces that light up so dimly and fleetingly in dreams. These forces fill the Cosmos, they are all-pervading. From them the human being derives the impulses through which, as he descends on to the Earth, he forms this body—the greatest work-of-art of the Macrocosm.

That which lights up so dimly in the dream—deserted, as it were, by the clear light of the sun—lives in the Spirit-world where the spiritual Sun flows through and through it, and where it waits until the Beings of the Hierarchies or man himself shall summon it to the creation of a new existence.

Further Leading Thoughts issued from the Goetheanum for the Anthroposophical Society

156. In Waking life, to experience *himself* in full and free Self-consciousness, man must forego the conscious experience of Reality in its true form, both in his existence and in that of Nature. Out of the ocean of Reality he lifts himself, that in his shadowed Thoughts he may make his own 'I' his very own in consciousness.

157. In Sleep, man lives with the life of his environment of Earth, but this very life extinguishes his consciousness of Self.

158. In Dreaming, there flickers up into half-consciousness the potent World-existence out of which the being of man is woven and from which, in his descent from Spirit-world, he builds his body. In earthly life this World-existence with its potent forces is put to death in man; it dies into the shadows of his Thought. For only so can it become the basis of self-conscious Manhood.

When the Mystery of Golgotha took place, the 'Gnosis' was the mode of thought of those among humanity who were able, already at that time, to understand this event—the most momentous in the earthly evolution of mankind—with an understanding not only of deep feeling but of clear knowledge.

To comprehend the mood of soul whereby the Gnosis lived in man, we must bear in mind that its age was the age of unfolding of the Intellectual or Mind-Soul. In this same fact we can discover the cause of the disappearance—well-nigh complete—of the Gnosis from human history. Till we can thus understand it, the disappearance of the Gnosis is, after all, one of the most astonishing occurrences in human evolution.

The unfolding of the Intellectual or Mind-Soul was preceded by that of the Sentient Soul, and this in turn by that of the Sentient Body. When the facts of the world are perceived through the Sentient Body, the whole of man's knowledge lives in his senses. He perceives the world coloured, resonant, and so forth; but within the colours and sounds, within the states of warmth, he knows the presence of a world of Spiritual Beings. He does not speak of 'substances,' of 'matter' to which the phenomena of colour, warmth, etc., are supposed to adhere, but of Spiritual Beings who manifest themselves through the perceptions of the senses.

In this age, there is as yet no special development of an 'intellect'—there is no intellect in man beside the faculty of sense-perception. Man either gives himself up with his own being to the outer world, in which case the Gods reveal themselves to him through the senses; or else in his soul-life he withdraws from the outer world and is then aware of a dim sense of life within.

But a far-reaching change takes place with the unfolding

of the Sentient Soul. The manifestation of the Divine through the senses grows dim and fades away. In place of it man begins to perceive the mere sense-impressions—colours, states of warmth, etc.—empty, as it were, of the Divine. And within him the Divine now manifests itself in a spiritual form, in pictorial ideas. He now perceives the world from two sides: through sense-impressions from without, and through Spirit-impressions of an ideal kind from within.

Man at this stage must come to perceive the Spirit-impressions in as definite a shape and clear a form as he hitherto perceived the divinely permeated sense-impressions. And indeed, while the age of the Sentient Soul holds sway he is still able to do this. For from his inner being the idea-pictures rise before him in a fully concrete shape. He is filled from within with a sense-free Spirit-content—itself an image of the contents of the World. The Gods, who hitherto revealed themselves to him in a garment of sense, reveal themselves now in the garment of the Spirit.

This was the age when the Gnosis really originated and had its life. It was a wonderful and living knowledge, in which man knew that he could share if he unfolded his inner being in purity and thus enabled the Divine content to manifest itself through him. From the fourth to the first millennium before the Mystery of Golgotha, this Gnosis lived in those portions of humanity which were most advanced in knowledge.

Then begins the age of the Intellectual or Mind-Soul. Of their own accord the World-pictures of the Gods no longer rise out of the inner being of man. Man himself must apply an inner force to draw them forth from his own soul. The outer world with all its sense-impressions becomes a question —a question to which he obtains the answers by kindling the inner force to draw forth the World-pictures of the Gods from within him. But these pictures are pale now, beside their former shape and character.

Such was the soul-condition of the portion of humanity

that evolved so wonderfully in ancient Greece. The Greek felt himself intensely in the outer world of the senses, wherein he also felt the presence of a magic power summoning his own inner force to unfold the World-pictures. In the field of Philosophy, this mood of soul came forth in Platonism.

But behind all this there stood the world of the Mysteries. In the Mysteries, such Gnosis as still remained from the age of the Sentient Soul was faithfully preserved. Human souls were definitely trained for this task of preservation. In the time when the Intellectual or Mind-Soul arose by way of ordinary evolution, the Sentient Soul was kindled into life by special training. Most especially in the age of the Intellectual or Mind-Soul, behind the ordinary life of culture there was a richly developed life of the Mysteries.

In the Mysteries the World-pictures of the Gods lived also in this way, that they were made the inner content of a cult or ritual. We gaze into the centres of those Mysteries and behold the Universe, portrayed in the most wonderful acts of ritual.

The human beings who experienced these things were also those who, when the Mystery of Golgotha took place, perceived and penetrated it in its deep, cosmic significance. But this life of the Mysteries was kept entirely apart from the turmoil of the outer world, in order to unfold in purity the world of Spirit-pictures. And it became increasingly difficult for the souls of men to unfold the pictures.

Then it was that in the highest places of the Mysteries, Spirit-beings descended from the spiritual Cosmos, coming to help the human beings in their intense strivings after knowledge. Thus under the influence of the 'Gods' themselves the impulses of the age of the Sentient Soul continued to unfold. There arose a 'Gnosis of the Mysteries' of which only the very few had any notion. And that which human beings were able to receive with the Intellectual or Mind-Soul was present alongside of this. It was the exoteric Gnosis whose fragments have come down to posterity.

In the esoteric Gnosis of the Mysteries, human beings grew less and less able to rise to the unfolding of the Sentient Soul. The esoteric Wisdom passed over more and more into the keeping of the Gods alone. *It is a great secret* of the historic evolution of humanity, that 'Divine Mysteries'—for as such we may indeed describe them—were at work in it from the first Christian centuries on into medieval times.

In these 'Divine Mysteries,' Angel-beings preserved in Earth-existence what human beings were no longer able to preserve. Thus did the Gnosis of the Mysteries hold sway, while men were diligently wiping out the exoteric Gnosis.

The *World-picture-content*, guarded in the Gnosis of the Mysteries by Spirit-beings in a spiritual way, while its influence was still required in the progress of mankind, could not, however, be preserved for the conscious understanding of man's soul. But its deep feeling-content had to be preserved. For in the right cosmic moment this was to be given to a humanity duly prepared to receive it, so that at a later stage the Spiritual Soul—fired by the inner warmth of it—might newly penetrate into the Spirit-realm. Thus, Spirit-beings built the bridge from the old World-content to the new.

Indications of this secret of human evolution do indeed exist. The sacred jasper cup of the Holy Grail which Christ made use of when He broke the bread and in which Joseph of Arimathea gathered the blood from the wound of Jesus—which contained therefore the secret of Golgotha—was received into safe keeping, according to the legend, by Angels until Titurel should build the Castle of the Grail, when they could allow it to descend upon the human beings who were prepared to receive it.

Spiritual Beings protected the World-pictures in which the secrets of Golgotha were living. And when the time was come, they let down—not the picture-content, for this was not possible—but the full Feeling-content, into the hearts and minds of men.

This implanting of the Feeling-content of an ancient knowledge can only serve to kindle, but it can indeed kindle most powerfully the unfolding in our age—out of the Spiritual Soul and in the light of Michael's activity—of a new and full understanding of the Mystery of Golgotha.

Anthroposophy strives for this new understanding, which—as we may see from the above description—cannot be a renewal of the Gnosis. For the content of the Gnosis was the way of knowledge of the Sentient Soul, while Anthroposophy—in a completely new way—must draw forth a content no less rich from the Spiritual Soul.

January, 1925

Further Leading Thoughts issued from the Goetheanum for the Anthroposophical Society (in connection with the above Study on Gnosis and Anthroposophy)

159. The Gnosis in its proper form evolved in the age of the Sentient Soul (from the fourth to the first millennium before the Mystery of Golgotha). It was an age when the Divine was made manifest to man as a spiritual content in his inner being; whereas in the preceding age (the age of the Sentient Body) it had revealed itself directly in his sense-impressions of the outer world.

160. In the age of the Intellectual or Mind-Soul, man could only experience in paler cast the spiritual content of the Divine. The Gnosis was strictly guarded in hidden Mysteries. And when human beings could no longer preserve it, because they could no longer kindle the Sentient Soul to life, spiritual Beings carried over—not indeed the Knowledge-content—but the Feeling-content of the Gnosis into the Middle Ages. (The Legend of the Holy Grail contains an indication of this fact.) Meanwhile the exoteric Gnosis, which penetrated into the Intellectual or Mind-Soul, was ruthlessly exterminated.

161. Anthroposophy cannot be a revival of the Gnosis. For the latter depended on the development of the Sentient Soul; while Anthroposophy must evolve out of the Spiritual Soul, in the light of Michael's activity, a new understanding of Christ and of the World. Gnosis was the way of Knowledge—preserved from ancient time—which, at the time when the Mystery of Golgotha took place, was best able to bring home this Mystery to human understanding.

THE FREEDOM OF MAN AND THE AGE OF MICHAEL

In the human faculty of memory there lives the personal image of a cosmic force—a cosmic force that worked upon the human being in the past, in the way revealed by our last studies. This cosmic force is still working at the present time. It works as the force of growth, as the life-giving impulse in the background of human life. The major portion of it works in this way, and only a small part is separated off as an activity that enters into the conscious Spiritual Soul, where it shows itself as the force of memory.

We must learn to see this force of memory in its true light. When in the present epoch of cosmic evolution a man perceives with his senses, his perception is a momentary lighting-up of world-*pictures* in consciousness. This lighting-up takes place when the senses are directed to the outer world. It illumines the consciousness and vanishes when the senses are no longer directed outward. That which lights up in the human soul in this way must not have duration. For if man did not eliminate it from his consciousness quickly enough, he would lose himself in this content of consciousness. He would no longer be himself. For a short time only—in the so-called 'after-images' in which Goethe was so interested—the inner illumination of a sense-perception may live on in consciousness. Nor must this content of consciousness crystallise into real being. It must remain a *picture*. It must on no account become real, any more than the picture in a looking-glass can become real.

Man would lose himself in anything that lived and worked itself out as a reality in his consciousness, just as he would lose himself in something which of its own nature possessed duration there. In this case, too, he could no longer be himself.

Thus our sense-perception of the outer world is an inward picture-painting by the human soul; a painting without materials; a painting in the ebb and flow—in the coming-into-being and the vanishing of Spirit. As in Nature a rainbow comes forth and passes away, leaving no trace behind, so does a perception arise and pass away, without *of its own inherent nature* leaving any memory behind.

But simultaneously with each perception another process takes its course between the soul of man and the outer world—a process lying in the more hidden portions of the soul-life, where the forces of growth, the life-impulses are at work. In this part of the soul's life, not only a fleeting image but a permanent and real image is impressed in every act of perception. Man can suffer this, for this is a part of the contents of the world, connected with his being. He cannot lose himself while this process is taking place, any more than he loses himself through the fact that he grows and is nourished without his own full consciousness.

This second process takes place in every act of outward perception. And when a man draws forth his memories from within him, it is an inward perception of that which has remained permanent through the second process.

Once again the soul paints a picture, but now it paints the past that is living in the man's own inner being. And once again, while he is thus painting, no lasting reality may form itself *in consciousness*, but only a picture that arises and vanishes again.

Such is the connection in the human soul between the forming of an idea in the act of perception and the remembering of it.

But the forces of memory are perpetually striving to be more than they can be if man is not to lose *himself* as a self-conscious being.

For the forces of memory are relics of the past in human evolution, and as such they come within the realm of Lucifer's power. Lucifer strives so to condense the impressions of the outer world in the human being that they may continuously shine as ideation in his consciousness.

This Luciferic striving would be crowned with success if it were not for the force of Michael which counteracts it. Michael's force does not allow that which is painted in the inner light to crystallise into real being, but keeps it in the state of a fleeting picture.

But the excess of force, which presses upward from within the human being through Lucifer's activity, will be transformed in this Age of Michael into the force of Spiritual Imagination. For gradually into the common intellectual consciousness of mankind there will enter the force of Imagination. But this does not mean that man will burden his present consciousness with lasting realities. His present consciousness will still be working in the fleeting pictures that arise and vanish. With his Imaginations, however, he reaches up into a higher Spirit-world, just as with his memories he reaches down into his own human nature. Man does not keep the Imaginations within him. They are drawn as cosmic pictures into cosmic existence and thence he is able to copy them, painting them again and again in his own life of picture-ideation.

Thus what Michael preserves from crystallisation in the inner being of man is received by the spiritual world. What man experiences of the force of conscious Imagination becomes at once a part of the World-contents. That this can be so, is an outcome of the Mystery of Golgotha. The Christ-force impresses the spiritual Imagination of man into the Cosmos. It is the Christ-force, united with the Earth. So long as it was not united with the Earth but worked upon the Earth as the Sun-force from without, all the impulses of life and growth went into the inner nature of man. He was formed and maintained by them, out of the Cosmos. Since the Christ-Impulse has been living with the Earth, man in his self-conscious being is given back again to the Cosmos.

From a cosmic being, man has become an earthly being. He has the potentiality to become a cosmic being once again, when as an earthly being *he has become himself.*

Thus in his momentary ideation or *forming of ideas* man lives not in an element of real being, but only in a mirroring of being—in a picture-being. In this fact the possibility of development of Freedom lies inherent. All that is *being* in consciousness has power to compel. But a *picture* cannot compel. If anything is to be brought about through the impression that the picture makes, it must happen quite independently of the picture. Man becomes free through the fact that with his Spiritual Soul he rises out of the ocean of being and emerges in the picture-existence *which has no being.*

Here the weighty question arises: Does not man lose hold of being altogether, inasmuch as he leaves it and plunges into non-being with a portion of his nature? This is another point where in our contemplation of the world we find ourselves face to face with one of the greatest riddles.

That which is experienced in consciousness as ideation, originated from the Cosmos. In relation to the Cosmos, man plunges into non-being. He *frees himself* in ideation from all the forces of the Cosmos. He paints the Cosmos while he himself is outside it.

If this were all, freedom would light up in the human being for a single cosmic moment, but in the very same moment the human being would dissolve away. But while in ideation man becomes free from the Cosmos, in his unconscious life of soul he is still organically connected with his former earthly lives, and his lives between death and a new birth. As a conscious man he is in the sphere of picture-being, while with his unconscious life he maintains himself within the spiritual reality. He experiences freedom in the *present* ego, while his *past* ego preserves him in the element of real being.

With respect to real being, man in his life of ideation is completely given to what he has become through the whole course of the cosmic and earthly past.

We are here pointing to the abyss of nothingness in human evolution which man must cross when he becomes a free being. It is the working of Michael and the Christ-Impulse which makes it possible for him to leap across the gulf.

Further Leading Thoughts issued from the Goetheanum for the Anthroposophical Society (with respect to the foregoing study: The Freedom of Man and the Age of Michael)

162. In ideation man lives not in Being, but in Picture-being—in a realm of Non-being—with his conscious Spiritual Soul. Thus is he freed from living and experiencing with the Cosmos. Pictures do not compel; Being alone has power to compel. And if man does direct himself according to the pictures, his doing so is independent of them, that is to say in freedom from the Universe.

163. In the moment of such ideation man is joined to the Being of the Universe by that alone which he has become through his own past: through his former lives on Earth, and lives between death and new birth.

164. Only through Michael's activity and the Christ-Impulse, can man achieve this leap across the gulf of Non-being in relation to the Cosmos.

WHERE IS MAN AS A BEING WHO THINKS AND REMEMBERS?

With his power to form ideas (thinking) and his experience of memories, man finds himself within the physical world. But wherever he may turn his gaze in this physical world, he will nowhere find with his senses anything that could give him the power to form ideas and to remember.

Self-consciousness appears in the act of forming ideas. This is, in accordance with our former studies, an acquisition man possesses from the forces of the Earth. But these earthly forces are such as remain concealed from the vision of the senses. During earthly life man thinks only that which his senses impart to him, but the power to think is not given him by anything of all that he thus thinks.

Where do we find this force which forms ideas (thought) and the pictures of memory out of that which belongs to the Earth?

We find it when the spiritual vision is directed to that which man brings with him from the previous Earth-lives. The ordinary consciousness knows nothing of this. It lives in man unconsciously at first; but when, after his spiritual life, man enters into earthly existence, it immediately shows itself to be related to those earthly forces which do not come into the sphere of sense-observation and sense-thought.

Man is not in this sphere with his ideas (thought), but with his will, which works in accordance with destiny.

When we consider that the Earth contains forces outside the sphere of the senses we may speak of the "spiritual Earth" as the opposite pole of the physical. It then follows that as a Willing being man lives in and with the "spiritual Earth," while as a Thinking being he is indeed within the physical Earth, but as such he does not live *with* it.

Man as a thinking being carries forces from the Spirit-world into the physical, but with these forces he remains a

Spirit-being who only appears in the physical world, but does not form a union with it.

The thinking human being forms a mutual relationship during earthly existence with the 'spiritual Earth' only; and out of this mutual relationship his self-consciousness develops. We therefore owe the development of self-consciousness to *spiritual* processes which take place in man during earthly life.

If with spiritual vision we grasp that which is here described, we have before us the 'human ego.'

With the experiences of memory we come into the sphere of the human astral body. In the act of remembering there stream into the present ego not merely the results of former Earth-lives, as is the case in thinking, but into his inner being stream the forces of the Spirit-world, which man experiences between death and new birth. This in-streaming takes place into the astral body.

Again there is no sphere within the physical Earth for the immediate reception of the forces which thus stream in. As a being who remembers, man cannot unite with the objects and processes perceived by his senses, any more than he can unite with them as a being who forms ideas.

But he forms a mutual relationship with that which is not indeed physical, but which transposes the physical into processes, into events. These are the rhythmical processes in Nature and in human life. In Nature, day and night alternate rhythmically, the seasons of the year follow in rhythmic succession, etc. In man, the processes of respiration and the circulation of the blood take place rhythmically; so do the alternating states of waking and sleeping, etc.

Rhythmical processes are nothing physical, either in Nature or in man. They might be called half spiritual. The physical as object vanishes in the rhythmic process. In the act of remembering, man's being is transposed into his own rhythm as well as into that of Nature. He lives in his astral body.

Indian Yoga wishes to submerge itself entirely in the experience of rhythm. It wishes to leave the sphere of thought, the sphere of the ego, and in an inward experience similar to memory look into the world that lies behind the one which it is possible for the ordinary consciousness to know.

It is not permissible for the spiritual life of the West to suppress the ego in order to 'know.' It must bring the ego ('I') to the perception of the Spiritual.

This cannot take place if we penetrate from the world of the senses to the world of rhythm, and so experience in the rhythm only the process in which the physical becomes half spiritual. Rather we must find that sphere of the Spirit-world which reveals itself in rhythm.

Two things are therefore possible. Firstly, the experience of the physical in the rhythmical element as the physical becomes half spiritual. This is an older path, one not to be followed any longer at the present time. Secondly, the experience of the Spirit-world, which possesses as its sphere the cosmic rhythm within man and without him, just as man's sphere is the earthly world with its physical beings and processes.

Now to this Spirit-world belongs everything that takes place at the present cosmic moment through Michael. A Spirit such as Michael brings that which otherwise would lie in the Luciferic sphere into the purely human evolution—which is not influenced by Lucifer—by choosing the world of rhythm for his dwelling-place.

All this can be seen when man enters into Imagination. For with Imagination the soul lives in rhythm, and Michael's world is the one which reveals itself in rhythm.

Memory stands already in this world, but not very deeply. The ordinary consciousness experiences nothing of it. But if we enter into Imagination there emerges first of all, out of the world of rhythm, the world of subjective memories; and this passes over at once into the archetypal pictures for the physical world which are created by the Divine-Spiritual world and which live in the etheric. We experience the ether which lights up in cosmic pictures and conceals within it the creative activity of the Universe. And the Sun-forces weaving in this ether are there not merely radiant, they conjure up the archetypal world-pictures out of the light. The Sun appears as the cosmic world-painter. It is the cosmic counterpart of the impulses which in man paint the pictures of thought.

(February, 1925)

Further Leading Thoughts issued from the Goetheanum for the Anthroposophical Society (in connection with the foregoing study: Where is man as a being who thinks and remembers?)

165. Man as a thinking being, though he lives in the realm of the physical Earth, does not enter into communion with it. He lives, a spiritual being, in such a way as to perceive the physical; but the forces for his Thinking, he receives from the 'spiritual Earth,' in the same way in which he receives his Destiny—the outcome of his former lives on Earth.

166. What he experiences in Memory is already within that world where in rhythm the physical becomes half spiritual, and where such Spirit-processes take place as are being brought about in the present cosmic moment by Michael.

167. He who learns to know Thinking and Memory in their true nature, will also begin to understand how man as an earthly being, though he lives within the earthly realm, does not become submerged in it with his full being. For as a being from beyond the Earth, he is seeking by communion with the spiritual Earth for his Self-consciousness—for the fulfilment of his Ego.

The Cosmos reveals itself to man, first of all, from the aspect of the Earth and from the aspect of what is outside the Earth, viz. the world of the stars.

Man feels himself related to the Earth and its forces. Life gives him very clear instruction regarding *this* relationship.

In the present age he does not feel himself related in the same way to the stars that are around him. But this lasts only so long as he is not conscious of his etheric body. To grasp the etheric body in Imaginations means to develop a feeling that we belong to the world of the stars, just as we have this feeling regarding the Earth through the consciousness of the physical body.

The forces which place the etheric body in the world come from the Cosmos *around* the Earth; those for the physical body radiate from the *centre* of the Earth.

But together with the etheric forces which stream to the Earth from the sphere of the Cosmos there come also the World-impulses which work in the astral body of man.

The ether is like an ocean in which the astral forces swim from all directions of the Cosmos and approach the Earth.

But in the present cosmic age only the mineral and plant kingdoms come into a direct relation to the astral, which streams down to the Earth on the waves of the ether; not the animal kingdom and not the human kingdom.

Spiritual vision shows that in the animal embryo there lives, not the astral that is now streaming to the Earth, but that which streamed in during the Old Moon period.

In the case of the plant kingdom we see how its manifold and wonderful forms are developed through the astral loosening itself from the ether and working over to the world of plants.

In the animal kingdom we see how, from out of the Spiritual, the astral which was active in very ancient times—during the Moon evolution—has been preserved, and works as something stored up and preserved, remaining on at the present time in the spirit-world, and not coming forth into the etheric world.

The activity of *this* astral is, moreover, mediated by the Moon-forces, which have likewise remained in the same condition, from the previous stage of the Earth.

In the animal kingdom we have, therefore, the result of impulses which manifested themselves externally in Nature in a previous stage of Earth-existence, whereas in the present cosmic age they have withdrawn into the Spirit-world which actively penetrates the Earth.

Now it is manifest to spiritual vision that within the animal kingdom only the astral forces which have been preserved in the present Earth from the former period are important for the permeation of the physical and etheric bodies with the astral body. But when the animal is once in possession of its astral body, the Sun-impulses appear actively in this astral body. The Sun-forces cannot give the animal anything astral; but when this is once in the animal, they must set to work and foster growth, nutrition, etc.

It is different for the human kingdom. This, too, receives its astrality to begin with from the Moon-forces that have been preserved. But the Sun-forces contain astral impulses which while they remain inactive for the animal kingdom, in the human astral continue to act in the same way in which Moon-forces worked when man was first permeated with astrality.

In the animal astral body we see the world of the Moon; in the human, the harmonious accord of the worlds of the Sun and Moon.

The fact that man is able to receive, for the development of self-consciousness, the Spiritual which rays forth in what belongs to the Earth, depends upon this which belongs to the Sun in the human astral body. The astral streams in from the sphere of the Universe. It acts either as astrality which pours in at the present time or as astrality which streamed in in ancient times and has been preserved. But everything that is connected with the shaping of the Ego as the vehicle of self-consciousness must radiate from the *centre* of a star. The astral works from the circumference; that which belongs to the Ego works from a centre. From its centre the Earth as a star gives the impulse to the human Ego. Every star radiates from its centre forces which mould or shape the Ego of some being.

This shows the polarity existing between the centre of a star and the sphere of the Cosmos.

From the above it may also be seen how the animal kingdom still stands there to-day as the result of former evolutionary forces of the Earth's being, how it uses up the astral forces which have been preserved, and how it must disappear when these have been consumed. Man, however, acquires new astral forces from that which belongs to the Sun. These enable him to carry on his evolution into the future.

From all this it may be seen that the nature of man cannot be understood unless we are just as conscious of his connection with the stars as of his connection with the Earth.

And that which man receives from the Earth for the unfolding of his self-consciousness depends also upon the Spirit-world active within all that belongs to the Earth. The circumstance that the Sun gives to man what he needs for his astral depends upon the activities which took place during the Old Sun period. At that time the Earth received the capacity to unfold the Ego-impulses of humanity. It is the Spiritual from that period which the Earth has preserved for itself from the Sun nature; and it is preserved from dying out through the present activity of the Sun.

The Earth was itself Sun at one time. Then it was spiritualised. In the present cosmic age, what belongs to the Sun works from outside. This continually rejuvenates the Spiritual which originated in ancient times and is now growing old. At the same time this which belongs to the Sun and acts in the present, preserves that which belongs to a former period from falling into what is Luciferic. For that which continues to work, without being received into the forces of the present, succumbs to Luciferic influences.

We may say that man's feeling of belonging to the Cosmos beyond the Earth is in this cosmic epoch so dim that he does not notice it within his consciousness. And it is not only dim, it is drowned by his feeling of belonging to the Earth. As man is obliged to find his self-consciousness in the elements of the Earth, he so grows together with them during the early part of the age of the Spiritual Soul, that they act upon him much more strongly than is compatible with the true course of his soul-life. Man is to a certain extent stupefied by the impressions of the world of the senses, and during this condition, thought which is free and has life in itself cannot rise within man.

The whole of the period since the middle of the nineteenth century has been a period of stupefaction through the impressions received by the senses. It is the great illusion of this age that the over-powerful life of the senses has been considered to be the right one—that life of the senses whose aim was to obliterate completely the life in the Cosmos beyond the Earth.

In this stupefaction the Ahrimanic Powers were able to unfold their being. Lucifer was repulsed by the Sun-forces more than Ahriman, who was able to evoke, especially in scientific people, the dangerous feeling that ideas are applicable only to the impressions of the senses. Thus it is exactly in these circles that one can find so little understanding for Anthroposophy. They stand face to face with the results of spiritual knowledge and try to understand them with their ideas. But these ideas do not grasp the Spiritual because the experience of the ideas is drowned by the Ahrimanic knowledge of the senses. And so they begin to fear that if they have anything to do with the results of spiritual investigation, they may fall into a blind belief in authority.

In the second half of the nineteenth century the Cosmos

beyond the Earth became darker and darker for human consciousness.

When man becomes able to experience ideas within himself once more, then, even when he does not support his ideas on the world of the senses, light will again meet his gaze from the Cosmos beyond the Earth. But this signifies that he will become acquainted with Michael in his own kingdom.

When once the Festival of Michael in autumn becomes true and inward, then this thought will arise in all sincerity in the mind of him who celebrates the festival, and it will live in his consciousness: *Filled with ideas, the soul experiences Spirit-Light, when sense-appearance only echoes in man like a memory.*

If man is able to feel this he will also be able, after his festive mood, to plunge again in the right way into the world of the senses. And Ahriman will not be able to injure him.

(March, 1925)

Further Leading Thoughts issued from the Goetheanum for the Anthroposophical Society (in connection with the foregoing study: Man in his macrocosmic Nature)

168. In the beginning of the age of the Spiritual Soul, man's sense of community with the Cosmos beyond the Earth grew dim. On the other hand—and this was so especially in men of science—his sense of belonging to the earthly realm grew so intense in the experience of sense-impressions, as to amount to a stupefaction.

169. While he is thus stupefied, the Ahrimanic powers work upon man most dangerously. For he lives in the illusion that the over-intense, stupefying experience of sense-impressions is the right thing and represents the true progress in evolution.

170. Man must find the strength to fill his world of Ideas with

light and to experience it so, even when unsupported by the stupefying world of sense. In this experience of the world of Ideas—independent and in their independence filled with light—his sense of community with the Cosmos beyond the Earth will re-awaken. Hence will arise the true foundation for festivals of Michael.

THE SENSE- AND THOUGHT-SYSTEMS OF MAN IN RELATION TO THE WORLD

When man first applies Imaginative Cognition to the contemplation of his own human being, he begins by eliminating his own sense-system from the field of vision. As he now observes himself, he becomes a being without the system of senses. Not that he ceases to have before his soul pictures such as were previously conveyed by the sense-organs. But he ceases to feel himself connected with the outer physical world through the sense-organs. The pictures of the outer physical world which he now has before his soul are no longer conveyed by the organs of sense. His very vision of them is proof of the fact that even through the sense-connection with the outer world of Nature, he has yet another connection with this world—one that does not depend on the senses. It is a connection with the Spirit that is embodied in the world of Nature.

In such vision, therefore, the physical world falls away from man. It is the earthly world that falls away. Man no longer feels this earthly world upon him.

It might be imagined that he would in the same moment lose self-consciousness. For this would seem to follow from our previous studies, which showed self-consciousness to be an outcome of the connection of man with the Earth-nature. But it is not so. Man preserves what he has gained through the earthly nature, even when, *after having gained it*, he divests himself of it in the conscious activity of higher knowledge.

By the above-described, spiritually Imaginative vision, the fact is revealed that man's sense-system is not, fundamentally speaking, at all intensely connected with his being. It is not really *he* who lives in this sense-system, but his environment. It is the outer world with *its* nature which has built itself into the sense-organisation of man.

Therefore, when he becomes an Imaginative seer, man really regards his sense-system as a portion of the outer world.

It is indeed closer to his being than the world of Nature around him; but still, it belongs to the outer world. It is only distinguished from the remaining outer world in this, that man can dive down into the latter with activity of knowledge through sense-perception and in no other way. Into his own sense-system, on the other hand, he dives down with conscious inner experience. The sense-system is a part of the outer world; but into this outer world man penetrates with his own being of soul-and-spirit, which he brings with him as he descends from the Spirit-world and enters Earth-existence.

Except for this fact that he fills it with his own being of soul-and-spirit, man's sense-system is of the outer world, just as is the plant kingdom that is spread around him. The eye in the last resort belongs to the world and not to man, just as the rose which man perceives belongs not to him, but to the world.

In the age of cosmic evolution that man has just passed through, thinkers arose who declared that colour, sound, warmth-impressions and the like were not really in the world, but in the human being. The 'red colour,' they say, is not anything at all out there in the world-environment of man; it is but the effect of an unknown reality upon him. But the very opposite of this conception is the truth. It is not the colour which, with the eye, belongs to man; it is the eye that with the colour belongs to the world. During his life on Earth man does not let the Earth-environment pour in upon himself, but *grows outward*—from birth to death—into this outer world.

It is significant that at the end of the Age of Darkness, when men stared out into the world without even dimly experiencing the light of the Spirit, the true idea of man's relationship to his environment was replaced by its very opposite.

When, in Imaginative Cognition, man has eliminated that environment in which he lives by means of his sense-system, there enters into the sphere of conscious experience another system—namely, that which is the bearer of his Thought, even as the sense-system is the bearer of his picture-world of sense-perception.

And now man knows himself to be connected through his thinking system with the cosmic environment of the stars, even as he previously knew himself to be connected through his sense-system with the Earth-environment. He now recognises himself as a cosmic being. His thoughts are no longer phantom-shadow pictures. They are saturated with reality, as sense-pictures are in the act of sense-perception. And if at this stage the knower passes on to Inspiration, he becomes aware that he can cast aside this world of which the thinking system is the bearer, just as he can cast aside the earthly. He sees that with his thinking system, too, he belongs, not to his own being, but to the world. He realises how the world-thoughts hold sway in him by means of his own thinking system. Here again he becomes aware that he thinks, not by receiving images of the world into himself, but by *growing outward* with his own thinking organisation into the Thinking of the world.

Both with respect to his sense-system and his thinking-system, man is *world.* The world builds itself into him. In sense-perception and in thought, he is not he himself, but part of the contents of the world.

Now into his thinking system man penetrates with his own being of soul-and-spirit, which belongs neither to the earthly world nor to the world of stars, but is of a wholly spiritual nature and thrives in man from life to life on Earth. This being of soul-and-spirit is accessible only to Inspiration.

Thus man steps out of the earthly and cosmic systems of his nature, to stand before himself as a being of pure soul-and-spirit through conscious Inspiration.

And in this being of pure soul-and-spirit he meets the life and law of his own destiny.

With the sense-system man lives in his physical body, with the thinking system in his etheric body. Both systems having been cast aside in living activity of knowledge, he finds himself in his astral body.

Every time man casts aside a portion of the nature which he has assumed, the content of his soul is indeed impoverished on the one hand; and yet on the other hand it is enriched. The physical body being eliminated, the beauty of the plant-world as the senses see it is before him no longer, save in a far paler form; but on the other hand the whole world of elemental beings dwelling in the plant-kingdom rises up before his soul.

Because this is so, the man of true spiritual knowledge has no ascetic attitude to what the senses can perceive. In the very spiritual experience, there remains alive in him the inner need to perceive once more through the senses what he now experiences in the Spirit. In the full human being, seeking as he does to experience the whole reality, sense-perception awakens the longing for its counterpart—the world of elemental beings. Likewise the vision of the elemental beings kindles the longing for the content of sense-perception once again.

Thus in the fullness of the life of man, Spirit longs for sense and sense for Spirit. There would be emptiness in spiritual existence, if the experiences of the conscious life in the senses were not there as a memory. There would be darkness in the life of sense-experience, if it were not for the active force of the Spirit which lights into it, albeit subconsciously at first.

Hence, when man will have made himself ripe to experience the activity of Michael, it will not mean that souls become impoverished in their experience of Nature. On the contrary, they will be enriched in this respect. And in the life of feeling, too, man will not tend to withdraw from sense-experience, but will be glad and eager to receive the wonders of this world of the senses more fully yet into his soul.

(March, 1925)

Further Leading Thoughts, issued from the Goetheanum (with regard to the foregoing study: The Sense- and Thought-Systems of Man, in relation to the World)

171. The organisation of the human senses belongs not to man's own nature, but is built into it by the outer world during his earthly life. Spatially though it is in man, in its real essence the perceiving eye is *in the World.* Man with his soul and spirit reaches out into that which the World is experiencing in him through his senses. He does not receive the physical environment into himself during his life on Earth, but grows out into it with his own soul and spirit.

172. Likewise his thinking organisation: through this he grows out into the existence of the stars. He knows himself as a world of stars; he lives and moves in the Cosmic Thoughts, when in the living experience of Knowledge he has put away the organisation of the senses.

173. When both are put away—the earthly world and the world of the stars as well—man stands before himself as a Being of soul and spirit. Here at length he is no longer *of the World*; here he is truly man. To become aware of what he experiences here, is *Self-knowledge*; even as it is *World-knowledge* to become aware in the organisation of the senses and of thought.

In sleep man is given up to the Cosmos. He carries out into the Cosmos that which he possesses as a result of former lives on Earth, when he descends from the world of soul-and-spirit into the earthly world. During his waking life he withdraws this content of his human being from the Cosmos.

In this rhythmic giving-himself-up to the Cosmos and withdrawing from it, man's life between birth and death takes its course.

While he withdraws it from the Cosmos, the soul-spiritual being of man is at the same time received by the system of nerves and senses. With the physical and life-processes that take place in the nerves-and-senses system, the soul-and-spirit of man combines in waking life, so that they work together unitedly. In this united action, sense-perception, the forming of memory-pictures and the play of fancy are contained. All these activities are bound to the physical body. The conceptions, the thinking experience—in which man becomes *conscious* of what is taking place half-consciously in perception, fancy and memory—are bound to the thinking system.

In this thinking organisation properly speaking, there also lies the region by which man experiences his self-consciousness. The thinking organisation is an organisation of the stars. If it lived and expressed itself *as such* alone, man would bear within him not a consciousness of self but a consciousness of the Gods. The thinking organisation is, however, lifted out of the Cosmos of the stars and transplanted into the realm of earthly processes. Man becomes a self-conscious being in that he experiences the world of stars within the earthly realm.

Here, therefore, we have the region of the inner life of man where the Divine-Spiritual world, united with the human being, sets him free in order that he may become Man in the fullest sense.

But directly beneath the thinking organisation—namely, where sense-perception, the play of fancy and the forming of memory, take place—the Divine-Spiritual world lives on within the life of man. We may say: it is in the unfolding of memory that the Divine-Spiritual lives in the waking state of man. For the other two activities, sense-perception and the play of fancy, are only modifications of the process that goes on in the forming of memory-pictures. In sense-perception we have the forming of a memory-content at the moment of its origin; in the content of fancy there lights up in the soul that of the content of memory which is preserved within the soul's existence.

Sleep carries over the soul-spiritual being of man into the cosmic world. With the activity of his astral body and his Ego, the sleeping man is steeped in the Divine-Spiritual Cosmos. He is not only outside the physical but outside the world of stars. But he is within the Divine-Spiritual Beings in whom his own existence has its origin.

In the present moment of cosmic evolution these Divine-Spiritual Beings work in such a way as to impress the moral content of the Universe into the astral body and Ego of man during sleep. All the World-processes in sleeping man are really moral processes, and cannot be spoken of as even remotely like the activities of Nature.

In their after-effects, man carries these processes over from sleeping into waking. But the after-effects remain asleep. For man is awake in that part of his life only which inclines to the sphere of Thought. What actually takes place in his sphere of Will is wrapped in darkness even in the waking state, as the whole life of the soul is wrapped in darkness during sleep. But in this sleeping life of the Will, the Divine-Spiritual works on in the waking life of man. Morally, man is as good or as bad as he can be according to the nearness with which he approaches the Divine-Spiritual Beings when asleep. And he comes nearer to them, or remains farther away from them, according to the moral quality of his former lives on Earth.

From the depths of the waking being of the soul's existence, that which was able to implant itself in the soul's existence, in community with the Divine-Spiritual world during sleep, sounds forth. *This is the voice of conscience.*

We see how the very things which a materialistic view of the world is most inclined to explain merely from the natural side, are found to lie on the moral side of things when seen by spiritual knowledge.

In *Memory* the Divine-Spiritual being works directly within the waking man. In *Conscience* the same Divine-Spiritual being works in the waking man indirectly—as an after-effect.

The forming of memory takes place in the organisation of nerves and senses. The forming of conscience takes place—albeit as a pure process of soul and spirit—in the metabolic and limbs-system.

Between the two there lies the rhythmic organisation, whose activity is polarised in two directions. In the breathing rhythm it is in intimate relation to sense-perception and to thought. In the breathing of the lung the process is at its coarsest. Thence it grows finer and finer, till, as a highly refined breathing process, it becomes sense-perception and thought.

Sense-perception is still very near to breathing; it is only a breathing through the sense-organs, not through the lungs. Thought, ideation, is farther removed from the lung-breathing, and is upheld by the Thinking system of man. And that which reveals itself in the play of fancy is already very close to the rhythm of blood-circulation. It is a very inward breathing, that comes into connection with the system of metabolism and the limbs. Psychologically, too, the activity of fancy reaches down into the sphere of Will, just as the circulatory system reaches down into the system of metabolism and the limbs.

In the activity of fancy, the thinking system comes close up to the system of the Will. The human being dives down into that sphere of his waking life which is asleep—the sphere of Will. Hence, in human beings who are especially developed in this direction, the contents of the soul appear like dreams in the waking state. Such a human organisation was present in Goethe. Goethe once said that Schiller must interpret to him his own poetic dreams.

In Schiller himself, a different human system was at work. He lived on the strength of what he brought with him from former lives on Earth. He had a strong life of the Will, and had to seek actively for the corresponding wealth of fancy.

The Ahrimanic Power, in its world-intentions, counts upon those human beings who are especially developed in the sphere of fancy—whose perception of sense-reality quite naturally transforms into the pictures of fancy. With the help of such human beings, the Ahrimanic Power hopes to be able to cut off the evolution of mankind from the past, and carry it on in the direction of its own, Ahrimanic intentions.

The Luciferic Power reckons on those human beings who, while naturally more developed in the sphere of Will, are inspired by an inner love for the ideal world-conception to transform their vision of sense-reality actively into pictures of creative fancy. Through such human beings the Luciferic Power would like to keep human evolution entirely within the impulses of the past. It would thus be able to preserve mankind from diving down into the sphere where the Ahrimanic Power must be overcome.

In this our earthly existence, we stand between two opposite poles. Above us spread the stars. From thence there radiate the forces which are connected with all things calculable and regular in Earth-existence. The regular alternation of day and night, the seasons, the longer cosmic periods, are the earthly reflection of the real process in the stars.

The other pole radiates out from the interior of the Earth. Irregular activities are at work in it. Wind and weather, thunder and lightning, earthquakes and volcanic eruptions, are a reflection of this process of the inner Earth.

Man himself is an image of this existence of the Stars and Earth. In his Thinking system lives the order of the Stars; in the Willing system of his limbs the chaos of the Earth. In the Rhythmic system he experiences in consciousness his own earthly being, in free balance and interplay between the two.

(March, 1925)

Further Leading Thoughts issued from the Goetheanum for the Anthroposophical Society (with regard to the foregoing study on Memory and Conscience)

174. Man is organised in spirit and in body from two different sides. First, from the physical-etheric Cosmos. Whatever radiates from the Divine-Spiritual Being into this organisation in man's nature, lives in it as the force of sense-perception, of the faculty of memory and of the play of fancy.

175. Secondly, man is organised out of his own past lives on Earth. This organisation is purely of the soul and spirit, and lives in him through the astral body and the Ego. Whatever enters of the life of Divine-Spiritual Beings into this human nature—its influence lights up in a man as the voice of conscience and all that is akin to this.

176. In his rhythmic organisation man has the constant union of the Divine-Spiritual impulses from the two sides. In life and experience of rhythm the force of memory is carried into the Willing life, and the might of conscience into the life in Ideas.

THE APPARENT EXTINCTION OF SPIRIT-KNOWLEDGE IN MODERN TIMES

To gain a true appreciation of Anthroposophy in relation to the development of the Spiritual Soul, we must turn our gaze again and again to the particular mental condition of civilised mankind which began with the blossoming forth of the Natural Sciences and reached its climax in the nineteenth century.

One should place the character of this age vividly before the soul's eye, comparing it with that of preceding ages. In all ages of the conscious evolution of mankind, Knowledge was regarded as that which brings man to the world of Spirit. To Knowledge, man ascribed whatever relationship to Spirit he possessed. Art and Religion were none other than the living life of Knowledge.

All this became different when the age of the Spiritual Soul began to dawn. With a very great part of the life of the human soul, Knowledge now concerned itself no more. Henceforth, it sought to investigate that relation to existence which man unfolds when he directs his senses and his intellectual judgment to the world of 'Nature.' It no longer wanted to concern itself with that which man unfolds as a relation to the world of Spirit, when he uses—not his outer senses—but his inner power of perception.

Thus there arose the necessity to connect the spiritual life of man, not with any living present Knowledge, but with Knowledge gained in the past—with Tradition.

The life of the human soul was rent in twain. On the one hand there stood before man the new science of Nature, striving ever onward and unfolding in the living present. On the other side there was the experience of a relation to the spiritual world, for which the corresponding Knowledge had arisen in the ages past. All understanding of *how* the Knowledge, corresponding to this side of human experience, had been gained in ages past, was gradually lost. Men possessed the Tradition, but they had lost the way by which the truths of Tradition had been *known*—discovered. All they could do now was to *believe* in the Tradition.

A man who had consciously reflected on the spiritual situation, say about the middle of the nineteenth century, would have been bound to admit: mankind has come to a point where it no longer feels itself capable of evolving any Knowledge, beyond that science which does not concern itself with the Spirit. Whatever can be known about the Spirit, a humanity of earlier ages was able to investigate and discover, but the human soul has lost the faculty for such discovery.

But men did not place before themselves the full bearing of what was taking place. They were content to say: Knowledge simply does not reach out into the spiritual world. The spiritual world can only be an object of Faith.

To gain some light upon these facts of modern history, let us look back into the time when the old Grecian wisdom had to retreat before the power of Rome, when Rome had accepted Christianity. When the last Greek Schools of the Philosophers were closed by the Roman Emperor, the last custodians of the ancient Knowledge too departed from the regions in which European spiritual life was henceforth to evolve. They found a haven in the Academy of Gondishapur in Asia, to which they now became attached. This was one of the centres of learning in the East where through the deeds of Alexander the tradition of the ancient Knowledge had been preserved.

The ancient Knowledge was living on there in the form which Aristotle had been able to give to it. But in the Academy of Gondishapur it was also taken hold of by that Oriental spiritual stream which we may describe as Arabism. Arabism, in one aspect of its nature, is a premature unfolding of the Spiritual Soul. Through the soul-life working prematurely in the direction of the Spiritual Soul, the possibility was given in Arabism for a spiritual wave to go forth, extending over Africa to southern and western Europe, and filling certain of the men of Europe with an intellectualism that should not properly have come until a later stage. In the seventh and eighth centuries, southern and western Europe received spiritual impulses which ought to have come only in the age of the Spiritual Soul.

This spiritual wave was able to awaken the intellectual life in man, but not the deeper founts of experience whereby the soul penetrates into the world of Spirit.

And now, when in the fifteenth to nineteenth centuries man exercised his faculty of Knowledge, he could but reach down to those levels of the soul where he did not yet impinge upon the spiritual world.

Arabism, entering into the spiritual life of Europe, held back the souls of men, in Knowledge, from the Spirit-world. Prematurely it brought that intellect into activity which was only able to apprehend the outer world of Nature.

This Arabism proved very powerful indeed. Whosoever was taken hold of by it, was seized by an inward—though for the most part quite unconscious—pride. He felt the power of intellectualism, but not the impotence of intellect by itself to penetrate into Reality. Thus he gave himself up to the externally given Reality of the senses, which places itself before the human being of its own accord. And it did not even occur to him to approach the spiritual Reality.

The spiritual life of the Middle Ages found itself face to face with this position. It possessed the sublime Traditions about the spiritual world. But the soul-life was intellectually so impregnated by the hidden influence of Arabism, that medieval Knowledge found no access to the sources from which the contents of the great Tradition had after all proceeded.

Thus from the early Middle Ages onwards, that which men felt instinctively within them as a connection with the Spirit, was battling with Thought in the form that this had assumed under Arabism.

Man felt the world of Ideas within him; he experienced it as something real. But he could not find the power in his soul to experience, in the Ideas, the Spirit. Thus arose *Realism*, feeling the reality in the Ideas and yet unable to discover it. In the world of the Ideas, Realism heard the speaking of the Cosmic Word, but it could not understand the speech. And *Nominalism* in opposition to it, seeing that the speech could not be understood, denied that there was any speech at all. For Nominalism, the world of Ideas was but a multitude of formulae within the human soul—rooted in no Reality of Spirit.

What lived and surged in these two currents, worked on into the nineteenth century. *Nominalism* became the mode of thought of Natural Science, which built up an imposing conceptual system of the outer world of sense, but destroyed the last relics of insight into the nature of the world of Ideas. *Realism* lived a dead existence. It knew still of the reality of the world of Ideas, but had no living Knowledge with which to reach it.

But man will reach it when Anthroposophy finds the way from the Ideas to *the living experience of Spirit in the Ideas*. In Realism truly carried forward, there will arise—side by side with the Nominalism of Natural Science—a path of Knowledge which will prove that the science of the Spiritual, far from being extinguished in mankind, can enter into human evolution once again, springing forth from newly-opened sources in the soul of man.

(March, 1925)

Further Leading Thoughts issued from the Goetheanum for the Anthroposophical Society (with regard to the foregoing study: The apparent Extinction of Spirit-Knowledge in Modern Time)

177. Looking with the eye of the soul upon the evolution of mankind in the Age of Science, a sorrowful perspective

opens up before us to begin with. Splendid grew the knowledge of mankind with respect to all that constitutes the outer world. On the other hand there arose a feeling as though a knowledge of the spiritual world were no longer possible at all.

178. It seems as though such knowledge had only been possessed by men of ancient times, and man must now rest content—in all that concerns the spiritual world—simply to receive the old traditions, making these an object of Faith.

179. From the resulting uncertainty, arising in the Middle Ages as to man's relation to the spiritual world, *Nominalism* and *Realism* proceeded. Nominalism is unbelief in the real Spirit-content of man's Ideas; we have its continuation in the modern scientific view of Nature. Realism is well aware of the reality of the Ideas, yet it can only find its fulfilment in Anthroposophy.

HISTORIC CATACLYSMS AT THE DAWN OF THE SPIRITUAL SOUL

The decline and fall of the Roman Empire and the appearance on the scene of peoples from the East—the great migrations—are a phenomenon of history to which the attention of true research must again and again be turned. For the present day still contains many an after-effect of these catastrophic happenings.

A true understanding of these events is impossible to merely exoteric history. For we must look into the souls of the human beings who took part in these migrations and witnessed the downfall of the Roman Empire.

Ancient Greece and Rome flourished in the epoch of human evolution when the Intellectual or Mind-Soul was unfolding. Indeed the Greeks and Romans were most essentially the bearers of this unfolding process. But in the Greek and Roman peoples the evolving of this stage of the soul did not contain the seed *from out of which* the Spiritual Soul could truly have developed. All the contents of soul and spirit, latent in the Intellectual or Mind-Soul, blossomed forth luxuriantly in the life of ancient Greece and Rome. But Greece and Rome were unable, out of their own inherent powers, to pass on to the new stage of the Spiritual Soul.

The stage of the Spiritual Soul did, of course, appear none the less. But the Spiritual Soul was as something implanted from without into the character of the Greek or Roman—something that did really not proceed out of the personality.

The connection with and severance from the Divine-Spiritual Beings, of which we have said so much in these studies, takes place with varying intensity in the course of succeeding ages. In olden times, it was a power entering into human evolution with the impulse of a mighty living process. In the Greek and Roman experience of the first Christian centuries it was a feebler power—but it still existed. While he was unfolding the fullness of the Intellectual or Mind-Soul within him, the Greek or Roman felt—unconsciously, but with no less deep a meaning for his soul—a loosening or severance from the Divine-Spiritual nature and a growing independence of the human. But this ceased in the first Christian centuries. The early dawn of the Spiritual Soul was felt as a renewed union, a closer connection with the Divine-Spiritual. Men evolved back again, from a greater to a lesser degree of independence of soul. Nor could they receive the Christian content into the human Spiritual Soul, for they were unable to receive the Spiritual Soul itself into their human being.

Thus they came to regard the Christian content as something given to them from outside—from the spiritual outer world—not as something with which they could become united through their own faculties of Knowledge.

But it was different with the peoples coming from the North-East, who now entered on the scene of history. They had passed through the stage of the Intellectual or Mind-Soul in a condition which, to them, conveyed a feeling of dependence on the spiritual world. They only began to feel something of human independence when, with the beginnings of Christianity, the earliest forces of the Spiritual Soul were dawning.

In them the Spiritual Soul appeared as something deeply bound up with the human being. They felt a glad sense of unfolding force within them when the Spiritual Soul was stirring into life.

It was into this new-springing life of the dawning Spiritual Soul that the Christian content entered in these peoples. They felt the Christian content as something springing to life within their souls, not as something given from outside.

Such was the mood in which these peoples approached the Roman Empire and all that was connected with it. Such was the mood of Arianism in contrast to Athanasianism. It was a deep inner conflict in world-historical evolution.

In the Spiritual Soul of the Greek and Roman, external as it was to man, there worked, to begin with, the Divine-Spiritual essence, not uniting fully with the earthly life, but raying into it from without. And in the Spiritual Soul of the Franks, the Germanic tribes, etc., which was only just dawning into life, such of the Divine-Spiritual as was able to unite with mankind worked as yet but feebly.

To begin with, the Christian content living in the Spiritual Soul that hovered over man grew and expanded in outer life. On the other hand, that Christian content which was united with the human soul, remained as an inner urge, an impulse within the human being waiting for future development—for a development which can only take place when a certain stage has been attained in the unfolding of the Spiritual Soul.

In the time from the first Christian centuries until the evolutionary epoch of the Spiritual Soul, the dominant spiritual life was a Spirit-content hovering above mankind—a content with which man was quite unable to unite himself in Knowledge. He therefore united with it in an outward way. He 'explained' it, and pondered on the question: how, and why, and to what degree the faculties of the soul were insufficient to bring about the full union with it in Knowledge. Thus he distinguished the realm into which Knowledge can penetrate, from that into which it cannot. It became the proper thing to renounce the exercise of those faculties of soul which rise with Knowledge into the spiritual world. And at length the time approached—the turn of the seventeenth and eighteenth centuries—in which the forces of the soul that inclined towards the Spirit were diverted from the Spiritual altogether, so far as active Knowledge was concerned. Men began to live their conscious life in those forces of the soul only, which are directed to the sense-perceptible.

Blunt indeed became the powers of Knowledge for spiritual things—most of all in the eighteenth century.

The thinkers of humanity now lost the spiritual content from their Ideas. In the Idealism of the first half of the nineteenth century, the Spirit-empty Ideas themselves are represented as the creative substance of the world. Thus Fichte, Schelling, Hegel. Or again, they point to a Supersensible which vanishes into thin air because it is bereft of Spirit. Thus Spencer, John Stuart Mill, and others. The Ideas are dead when they no longer seek the living Spirit.

There is no escaping the fact, lost was the sense of spiritual vision for the things of the Spirit. A 'continuation' of the old life of spiritual Knowledge is impossible. With the Spiritual Soul unfolding within him, man's faculties of soul must strive onward to reach their new union with the Spirit-world, a union elementary, immediate and living. Anthroposophy would fain be such a striving.

In the spiritual life of this age, it is just the leading personalities who to begin with do not know what Anthroposophy intends. Wide circles of people who follow in their wake are thereby kept away from Anthroposophy. The leading people of to-day live in a soul-content which in the course of time has grown altogether unaccustomed to use the spiritual forces. For them, it is as though one would call upon a man having an organ paralysed, to use it. Paralysed were the higher faculties of Knowledge from the sixteenth into the latter half of the nineteenth century. And mankind remained utterly unconscious of the fact; indeed, the one-sided application of Knowledge-powers directed to the outer world of sense was regarded as a sign of special progress.

(March, 1925)

Further Leading Thoughts issued from the Goetheanum for the Anthroposophical Society (with reference to the foregoing study: Historic Cataclysms at the Dawn of the Spiritual Soul)

180. The Greeks and Romans were the peoples predestined by their very nature for the unfolding of the Intellectual or Mind-Soul. They developed this stage of the soul to perfec-

tion. But they did not bear within them the seeds of a direct, unbroken progress to the Spiritual Soul. Their soul-life went under in the Intellectual or Mind-Soul.

181. In the time from the origin of Christianity until the age of the unfolding of the Spiritual Soul, a world of the Spirit was holding sway which did not unite with the forces of the human soul. The latter contrived to 'explain' the world of the Spirit, but they could not experience it in living consciousness.

182. The peoples advancing from the North-East in the great migrations, encroaching on the Roman Empire, took hold of the Intellectual or Mind-Soul more in the inner life of feeling. Meanwhile, imbedded in this element of feeling, the Spiritual Soul was evolving within their souls. The inner life of these peoples was waiting for the present time, when the re-union of the soul with the world of the Spirit is fully possible once more.

The Age of Philosophy is often said to have been superseded, about the middle of the nineteenth century, by the rising Age of *Natural Science*. And it is said that the Age of Natural Science still continues in our day, although many people are at pains to emphasise at the same time that we have found our way once more to certain philosophic tendencies.

All this is true of the paths of knowledge which the modern age has taken, but not of its *paths of life*. With his conceptions and ideas, man still lives in Nature, even if he carries the mechanical habit of thought into his Nature-theories. But with his life of Will he lives in the mechanical processes of technical science and industry to so far-reaching an extent, that it has long imbued this Age of Science with an entirely new quality.

To understand human life we must consider it to begin with from two distinct aspects. From his former lives on Earth, man brings with him the faculty to conceive the Cosmic—the Cosmic that works inward from the Earth's encircling spheres, and that which works within the Earth-domain itself. Through his senses he perceives the Cosmic that is at work upon the Earth; through his thinking organisation he conceives and thinks the Cosmic influences that work downward to the Earth from the encircling spheres.

Thus man lives, through his physical body in Perception, through his etheric body in Thought.

That which takes place in his astral body and his ego holds sway in the more hidden regions of the soul. It holds sway, for example, in his destiny. We must, however, look for it, to begin with, not in the complicated relationships of destiny, but in the simple and elementary processes of life.

Man connects himself with certain earthly forces, in that he gives his body its right orientation within them. He learns to stand and walk upright; he learns to place himself with arms and hands into the equilibrium of earthly forces.

Now these are *not* forces working inward from the Cosmos. They are forces of a *purely* earthly nature.

In reality, nothing that man experiences is an abstraction. He only fails to perceive whence it is that an experience comes to him; and thus he turns ideas about realities into abstractions. He speaks of the laws of mechanics. He thinks he has abstracted them from the connections and relationships of Nature. But this is not the case. All that man experiences in his soul by way of purely mechanical laws, has been discovered inwardly through his relationship of orientation to the earthly world (in standing, walking, etc.).

The Mechanical is thus characterised as that which is of a purely earthly nature. For the laws and processes of Nature as they hold sway in colour, sound, etc., have entered into the earthly realm from the Cosmos. It is only within the earthly realm that they too become imbued with the mechanical element, just as is the case with man himself, who does not confront the mechanical in his conscious experience until he comes within the earthly realm.

By far the greater part of that which works in modern civilisation through technical Science and Industry—wherein the life of man is so intensely interwoven—is *not Nature at all, but Sub-Nature.* It is a world which emancipates itself from Nature—emancipates itself in a downward direction.

Look how the Oriental, when he strives towards the Spirit, seeks to get out of the conditions of equilibrium whose origin is merely in the earthly realm. He assumes an attitude of meditation which brings him again into the purely Cosmic balance. In this attitude the Earth no longer influences the inner orientation of his body. (I am not recommending this for imitation; it is mentioned merely to make our present subject clear. Anyone familiar with my writings will know how different is the Eastern from the Western spiritual life in this direction.)

Man needed this relation to the purely earthly for the unfolding of his Spiritual Soul. Thus in the most recent times there has arisen a strong tendency to realise in all things, and even in the life of action, this element into which man must enter for his evolution. Entering the purely earthly element, he strikes upon the Ahrimanic realm. With his own being he must now acquire a right relation to the Ahrimanic.

But in the age of Technical Science hitherto, the possibility of finding a true relationship to the Ahrimanic civilisation has escaped man. He must find the strength, the inner force of knowledge, in order not to be overcome by Ahriman in this technical civilisation. He must understand Sub-Nature for what it really is. This he can only do if he rises, in spiritual knowledge, at least as far into extra-earthly Super-Nature as he has descended, in technical Sciences, into Sub-Nature. The age requires a knowledge transcending Nature, because in its inner life it must come to grips with a life-content which has sunk far beneath Nature—a life-content whose influence is perilous. Needless to say, there can be no question here of advocating a return to earlier states of civilisation. The point is that man shall find the way to bring the conditions of modern civilisation into their true relationship—to himself and to the Cosmos.

There are very few as yet who even feel the greatness of the spiritual tasks approaching man in this direction. Electricity, for instance, celebrated since its discovery as the very soul of Nature's existence, must be recognised in its true character—in its peculiar power of leading down from Nature to Sub-Nature. Only man himself must beware lest he slide downward with it.

In the age when there was not yet a technical industry independent of true Nature, man found the Spirit *within* his view of Nature. But the technical processes, emancipating themselves from Nature, caused him to stare more and more fixedly at the mechanical-material, which now became for him the really scientific realm. In this mechanical-material domain, all the Divine-Spiritual Being connected with the origin of human evolution, is completely absent. The purely Ahrimanic dominates this sphere.

In the Science of the Spirit, we now create another sphere in which there is no Ahrimanic element. It is just by receiving in Knowledge this spirituality to which the Ahrimanic powers have no access, that man is strengthened to confront Ahriman *within the world.*

(March, 1925)

Further Leading Thoughts issued from the Goetheanum for the Anthroposophical Society (with reference to the foregoing study: From Nature to Sub-Nature)

183. In the age of Natural Science, since about the middle of the nineteenth century, the civilised activities of mankind are gradually sliding downward, not only into the lowest regions of Nature, but even *beneath Nature.* Technical Science and Industry become Sub-Nature.

184. This makes it urgent for man to find in conscious experience a knowledge of the Spirit, wherein he will rise as high above Nature as in his sub-natural technical activities he sinks beneath her. He will thus create within him the inner strength *not to go under.*

185. A past conception of Nature still bore within it the Spirit with which the source of all human evolution is connected. By degrees, this Spirit vanished altogether from man's theory of Nature. The purely Ahrimanic spirit has entered in its place, and passed from theory of Nature into the technical civilisation of mankind.

Rudolf Steiner

GUIDANCE IN ESOTERIC TRAINING

From the Esoteric School

Selected from the material given by Rudolf Steiner to members of his Esoteric School (1904–14), this volume features exercises, meditations and practices for spiritual self-development. In contrast to oriental methods of spiritual training, they derive from the Western, Rosicrucian stream and are fully adapted to modern consciousness.

Various exercises are given, for morning and evening and for the days of the week and the months of the year. In addition, there is much explanatory material to deepen and enhance meditative work, including several articles on the path of inner development and the obstacles to be faced on the attainment of true consciousness of self. This enlarged edition contains further clarification of the exercises, descriptions of the future evolution of the world and humanity, plus later advice given by Steiner on the nature of breathing exercises and ancient and modern methods of initiation.

RUDOLF STEINER PRESS
192 pages; ISBN 1 85584 076 6; £10.95

Rudolf Steiner

SELF-TRANSFORMATION

At the heart of Rudolf Steiner's spiritual philosophy is the esoteric path of inner development that can lead to true self-transformation. In these lectures, Steiner shows how—by developing certain qualities such as clear thinking, inner tranquillity and positivity, as well as through meditative exercises—it is possible to break out of the shadowy, brain-bound world of everyday consciousness. The first step on this path of transformation is the level of Imagination, where the spiritual world is seen in pictures. Steiner indicates how one can then attain to the levels of Inspiration, and finally to the highest stage of Intuition.

As a highly-trained clairvoyant, Rudolf Steiner speaks on this question from his own spiritual experience. In contrast to many of the New Age paths available today, however, his methods are based on the western tradition, the Rosicrucian path of initiation, as opposed to older Eastern teachings. This modern path is, he suggests, a metamorphosis of the Eastern paths, and is best suited to modern consciousness.

Florin Lowndes

ENLIVENING THE CHAKRA OF THE HEART

The Fundamental Spiritual Exercises of Rudolf Steiner

While meditation is the foundation of any spiritual path of development, the seer and teacher Rudolf Steiner advised that specific 'accompanying', or 'fundamental', spiritual exercises should *always* be carried out in conjunction with it, in order to protect the individual from dangers posed to normal consciousness through the practise of meditation. The exercises offer this protection by helping to develop inner certainty and strength. This is achieved, for example, through the first exercise by concentrating and intensifying the powers of thinking, through the second by developing the control of the will, through the third by mastering the outer expressions of the life of feeling, and so on.

Florin Lowndes describes the fundamental exercises in thorough detail, giving suggestions as to how they can be carried out. He also relates an important and hidden aspect—that the exercises embody the means for developing and strengthening organic and 'living' thinking, which is intimately related to the enlivening of a new organ of perception: the heart chakra or lotus. Lowndes casts new light on many aspects of this question, and offers encouragement and stimulus to those seeking a modern path of spiritual development.

SOPHIA BOOKS (RUDOLF STEINER PRESS)
208 pages; ISBN 1 85584 091 X; £10.95